ECONOMIC ISSUES, PROBLEMS AND PERSPECTIVES

# INFLATION AND THE CONSUMER PRICE INDEX

## COSTS AND CONSIDERATIONS

# Economic Issues, Problems and Perspectives

Additional books in this series can be found on Nova's website under the Series tab.

Additional E-books in this series can be found on Nova's website under the E-books tab.

# America in the 21st Century: Political and Economic Issues

Additional books in this series can be found on Nova's website under the Series tab.

Additional E-books in this series can be found on Nova's website under the E-books tab.

ECONOMIC ISSUES, PROBLEMS AND PERSPECTIVES

# INFLATION AND THE CONSUMER PRICE INDEX

## COSTS AND CONSIDERATIONS

ETHAN L. GREEN
AND
AMBER N. WALKER
EDITORS

Nova Science Publishers, Inc.
*New York*

For permission to use material from this book please contact us:
Telephone 631-231-7269; Fax 631-231-8175
Web Site: http://www.novapublishers.com



Additional color graphics may be available in the e-book version of this book.

**Library of Congress Cataloging-in-Publication Data**

ISBN 978-1-61942-705-1

*Published by Nova Science Publishers, Inc. † New York*

# CONTENTS

# PREFACE

Since the end of World War II, the United States has experienced almost continuous inflation - the general rise in the price of goods and services. The costs of inflation are related to its rate, the uncertainty it engenders, whether it is anticipated, and the degree to which contracts and the tax system are indexed. A major cost is related to the inefficient utilization of resources because economic agents mistake changes in nominal variables for changes in real variables and act accordingly. This book examines the causes, costs, and current status to the economy from inflation with a focus on the Consumer Price Index; food price inflation and consumers; and inflation-indexing elements in federal entitlement programs.

Chapter 1- Since the end of World War II, the United States has experienced almost continuous inflation— the general rise in the price of goods and services. It would be difficult to find a similar period in American history before that war. Indeed, prior to World War II, the United States often experienced long periods of deflation. It is worth noting that the Consumer Price Index (CPI) in 1941 was virtually at the same level as in 1807.

During the last two economic expansions, March 1991-March 2001 and November 2001- December 2007, the inflation rate remained low by the standards of previous decades, and has remained low since this recession began. This is true regardless of which index is used to calculate the rate at which the price of goods and services rose. A low inflation rate is especially significant since the U.S. economy was fully employed, if not over fully employed, according to many estimates for the last three years of the 1991-2001 expansion and during 2006-2007. Yet, contrary to expectations, the inflation rate accelerated only modestly. Keeping an economy moving along a full employment path without igniting a burst of inflation is a difficult policy task.

Chapter 2- The Consumer Price Index (CPI) is perhaps the most widely reported measure of inflation. A number of federal government programs are regularly adjusted to account for changes in the CPI, such as Social Security benefits and the personal income tax rate schedule. Thus, the behavior of the CPI has important consequences for a large number of people. Many, however, may be unfamiliar with how the CPI is estimated.

For Congress, the CPI is of particular interest because of its significant effect on the federal budget. Changes in the CPI can have substantial effects on both revenues and outlays, and those changes may either reflect underlying economic conditions or result from methodological changes in the way the CPI is calculated.

Chapter 3- Inflation measures the rate of change in all prices. Maintaining low and stable inflation is one of the primary goals of macroeconomic policy. But how should inflation be measured? Policymakers, particularly at the Federal Reserve, often refer to *core* inflation in their policy decisions. Core inflation is commonly defined as a measure of inflation that omits changes in food and energy prices. Some policymakers prefer to use core inflation to predict future overall inflation because food and energy price volatility makes it difficult to discern trends from the overall inflation rate. A drawback of an over-reliance on core inflation, however, is that an extended period of rapidly rising food or energy prices could cause all other prices to accelerate. A focus on core may cause policymakers to fail to react to such a rise in inflation until it is too late. This scenario may have occurred recently. Many economists are concerned that rapid increases in food and energy prices are now pushing overall inflation to uncomfortably high levels. Furthermore, several studies have failed to find core inflation to be a good forecaster of future inflation, casting doubt on the very rationale for relying on it.

Chapter 4- The heightened commodity price volatility of 2008 and 2010 and the subsequent acceleration in U.S. food price inflation associated with those market shifts raised concerns and generated many questions about farm and food price movements by Members of Congress and their constituents. This report responds to those concerns by addressing the nature and measurement of retail food price inflation.

During the 1991 to 2006 period, U.S. food prices were fairly stable—annual food price inflation, as measured by the U.S. Bureau of Labor Statistics (BLS) Consumer Price Index (CPI) for all food (excluding alcoholic beverages), averaged a relatively low 2.5%. However, several economic factors emerged in late 2005 that began to gradually push market prices higher for both raw agricultural commodities and energy costs, and ultimately retail food prices. U.S. food price inflation increased at a rate of 4% in 2007 and at 5.5% in 2008—the highest since 1990 and well above the general inflation rate of 3.8%.

Chapter 5- In recent months, various proposals have been discussed in the context of ways to reduce federal budget deficits. One of the proposals, for example, is the use of a different measure of consumer price change to index various provisions of federal programs, including cost-of-living adjustments (COLAs). For example, under current law, the Social Security COLA is based on the Consumer Price Index for Urban Wage Earners and Clerical Workers (CPI-W). Under the proposal, the Social Security COLA would be based instead on the Chained Consumer Price Index for All Urban Consumers (Chained CPI-U or C-CPI-U). Because the goal of the Chained CPI-U is to better reflect how consumers change their buying habits in response to changes in prices, supporters of the proposal argue that it is a more accurate measure for computing COLAs and making other automatic program adjustments. Because the Chained CPI-U typically has risen more slowly than either the CPI-W or the "regular" CPI-U, however, opponents view the proposal as a backdoor way of reducing benefits. Some observers point out that the Chained CPI-U is published as a preliminary value that is subject to revision over a period of more than two years, and that it may not accurately reflect the cost of living for certain groups, such as the elderly population.

Chapter 6- The federal government, in an effort to protect the purchasing power of Social Security beneficiaries, indexes benefits to increases in the Consumer Price Index for Urban Wage Earners and Clerical Workers (CPI-W). Concern has periodically been expressed that the CPI-W may understate the impact of inflation on the elderly population and that it therefore may not be the most appropriate measure of inflation's impact on the elderly.

At the behest of Congress, the U.S. Bureau of Labor Statistics (BLS) developed an experimental price index to track changes in the cost of living for the population aged 62 and older. The average annual rate of change between December 1982 and December 2010 in the experimental consumer price index (CPI-E) for the elderly was 3.1%. Over the same period, the CPI-W rose by 2.9%. Methodological limitations in the experimental index may have contributed to this difference, however. Were BLS to construct an index that is more representative of the elderly population, there is no guarantee that the relationship between the new index and the CPI-W would be the same.

Chapter 7- The U.S. Bureau of Labor Statistics (BLS) publishes two important measures of inflation: the Consumer Price Index for all Urban Consumers (CPI-U) and the Consumer Price Index for Urban Wage Earners and Clerical Workers (CPI-W). The CPI might seem like just another economic indicator, but it could be a powerful policy lever. Because the CPI-W is used to calculate annual cost-of-living adjustments (COLAs) to Social Security retirement benefits and the CPI-U is used to calculate annual inflation adjustments to personal income tax brackets, for example, changing the basis of the automatic adjustments could substantially affect outlays and revenues, and thereby, the budget deficit.

As part of its continuing effort to improve measures of change in the cost of living, BLS has since August 2002 been publishing a supplemental measure known as the Chained Consumer Price Index for all Urban Consumers (C-CPI-U). The aim of the C-CPI-U is to produce a measure of change in consumer prices that is free of substitution bias.

Chapter 8- Federal laws try to protect taxpayers and recipients of government benefits from the effects of rising prices by specifying that dollar amounts in many parts of the tax code and in some programs be automatically adjusted— or indexed—for inflation. Without such indexing, a rise in the general level of prices would alter the effects of federal policies even in the absence of action by lawmakers. For example, if the dollar amounts that delineate the different tax brackets in the individual income tax were not indexed, inflation would push many people's income into higher brackets and boost average tax rates over time, even if income did not grow faster than prices.

Many federal programs and parts of the tax code are currently indexed to increases in the consumer price index (CPI), a measure of inflation calculated by the Bureau of Labor Statistics (BLS).[1] According to many analysts, however, the CPI overstates increases in the cost of living because it does not fully account for the fact that consumers generally adjust their spending patterns as some prices change relative to other prices. One option for lawmakers would be to link federal benefit programs and tax provisions to another measure of inflation—the chained CPI—that is designed to account fully for changes in spending patterns. The chained CPI grows more slowly than the traditional CPI does: by an average of 0.3 percentage points per year over the past decade. As a result, using that measure to index benefit programs and tax provisions would reduce federal spending (especially on Social Security and federal pensions) and increase revenues.

In: Inflation and the Consumer Price Index ISBN: 978-1-61942-705-1
Editors: E. L. Green, A. N. Walker 

*Chapter 1*

# INFLATION: CAUSES, COSTS, AND CURRENT STATUS*

*Marc Labonte*

## SUMMARY

Since the end of World War II, the United States has experienced almost continuous inflation— the general rise in the price of goods and services. It would be difficult to find a similar period in American history before that war. Indeed, prior to World War II, the United States often experienced long periods of deflation. It is worth noting that the Consumer Price Index (CPI) in 1941 was virtually at the same level as in 1807.

During the last two economic expansions, March 1991-March 2001 and November 2001- December 2007, the inflation rate remained low by the standards of previous decades, and has remained low since this recession began. This is true regardless of which index is used to calculate the rate at which the price of goods and services rose. A low inflation rate is especially significant since the U.S. economy was fully employed, if not over fully employed, according to many estimates for the last three years of the 1991-2001 expansion and during 2006-2007. Yet, contrary to expectations, the inflation rate accelerated only modestly.

* This is an edited, reformatted and augmented version of a Congressional Research Service publication, CRS Report for Congress RL30344, from www.crs.gov, dated July 26, 2011.

Keeping an economy moving along a full employment path without igniting a burst of inflation is a difficult policy task.

Because labor costs make up nearly two-thirds of total production costs, the rate at which they rise is often regarded as an indication of future inflation at the retail level. They tended to rise in the latter stage of the 1991-2001 expansion and to moderate during the subsequent contraction, recovery, and expansion that ended in December 2007.

Rather than measure inflation by using the rate at which prices overall are rising, some economists prefer a measure that reflects primarily the systematic factors that raise prices. This yields the "underlying" or "core" rate of inflation. Price increases over this period have been especially sharp in food and energy, which are not included in the core rate.

Why should the United States be concerned about inflation? This study reports the distilled knowledge of economists on the real cost to an economy from inflation. These are remarkably more varied than the outlays for "shoe leather," long reported to be the major cost of inflation ("shoe leather" being a shorthand term for the resources that have to be expended on less efficient methods of exchanges).

The costs of inflation are related to its rate, the uncertainty it engenders, whether it is anticipated, and the degree to which contracts and the tax system are indexed. A major cost is related to the inefficient utilization of resources because economic agents mistake changes in nominal variables for changes in real variables and act accordingly (the so-called signal problem). Inflation in the United States during the post-World War II era may not have been high enough for this cost to be significant.

## INTRODUCTION

Inflation—the general rise in the prices of goods and services—is one of the differentiating characteristics of the U.S. economy in the post-World War II era. Except for 1949, 1955, and 2009, the prices of goods and services have, on average, risen each year since 1945. The cumulative effect of this inflation is staggering: the price level has risen more than 1,000% since the end of World War II.[1] Inflation rose in the 1960s, peaked in the 1970s and early 1980s, and has been generally low but positive since then.

This was not true in the pre-World War II period. On the eve of that war, 1941, the U.S. price level was virtually the same as in 1807. During the periods from 1846 to 1861 and 1884 to 1909, the United States experienced a near constant price level. And in the 15 years from 1865 through 1879, the price level either remained constant or declined. The principal periods of inflation between 1800 and 1941 were associated with wars and the discoveries of gold and silver both here and abroad (and with increased efficiencies in extracting both metals).

## INFLATION DEFINED

Inflation can be defined as a sustained or continuous rise in the general price level or, alternatively, as a sustained or continuous fall in the value of money. Several things should be noted about this definition. First, inflation refers to the movement in the general level of prices. It does not refer to changes in one price relative to other prices. These changes are common even when the overall level of prices is stable.[2] Second, the prices are those of goods and services, not assets. Third, the rise in the price level must be somewhat substantial and continue over a period longer than a day, week, or month.[3]

## CAUSES OF INFLATION

There has been practically no period in American history in which a significant change in the price level has occurred that was not simultaneously accompanied by a corresponding change in the supply of money.[4] This has led to a widely held view that "inflation is always and everywhere a monetary phenomenon resulting from and accompanied by a rise in the quantity of money relative to output."[5]

Although this view is generally accepted, it is, in fact, consistent with two quite different views as to the cause of inflation.

In one view a more rapid rate of money growth plays an active role in inflation and results either from mistaken policies of the Federal Reserve or because the Federal Reserve subordinates itself to the fiscal requirements of the federal government and finances budget deficits through money creation. Examples of Federal Reserve policies that are likely to produce inflation are those that fix rates of interest too low or that support unrealistic foreign exchange values of the dollar. According to this view, the control of inflation rests with the Federal Reserve (Fed) and depends upon its willingness to limit the growth in the money supply.[6]

Because of this relationship, some economists are concerned about the rapid growth in the portion of the money supply controlled by the Fed (called the monetary base) from 2008 to 2011, although to date the rise in the monetary base has not been accompanied by a proportionate increase in the broader money supply, mainly because of the large slack in the economy at the time.[7]

An alternative view comes in several versions. They have in common a belief that the major upward pressure on prices comes from activities which would produce a fall in real output. A favorite candidate is the attempt by organized labor to obtain increases in real wages. Other activities include the monopolistic pricing behavior of OPEC, major crop failures or changes in the terms of international trade produced by a decline in the foreign exchange value of the dollar.

The decline in real output that these activities produce will, in general, lead to rises in unemployment. To prevent unemployment from increasing, in one version of this alternative, the Federal Reserve is seen to pump up demand by easing the growth of money and credit. In the process it ratifies the rise in the price level. Thus, in this version, while a growth in the money supply is necessary to ratify the upward movement in the price level, it is not the cause of the rise in prices.

It is interesting to speculate what would happen if the Federal Reserve refused to expand demand in the face of the rise in unemployment. Presumably, after a protracted period, the additional unemployment would lead to a fall in wages, costs, and other prices. Over the longer run, output would return to its previous level or growth path, the price level would fall back to its previous level and only relative prices and wages would be different. Thus, while the Federal Reserve has the power to curb inflation, it is unlikely to exercise this power in the face of a large run up in unemployment.

In another extreme variant, what the Federal Reserve does is really irrelevant. Should it refuse to expand what is conventionally called money to pump up demand in the presence of these developments that reduce output, money substitutes under the guise of credit will emerge that will allow demand to grow and the price increases to be ratified.

This variation, interestingly, precludes excessive money growth from causing inflation, for it also holds that the Federal Reserve cannot force too much money on the economy. Inflation, then, cannot be a case in which too much money is chasing too few goods.[8]

The first two explanations for inflation find many adherents among American economists, whereas the third is more common among some British economists.

## The Relationship between Inflation and Unemployment

In most years, inflation tends to rise when unemployment falls, and vice versa. Economic theory explains this relationship in terms of a full employment rate of unemployment, also called the natural rate of unemployment or the non-accelerating inflation rate of unemployment (NAIRU).[9] Whenever the actual unemployment rate is above the full employment rate, total spending in the economy will fall, and the resultant slack will cause the inflation rate to fall (since there is less demand for goods and services). As the inflation rate falls, the expected rate of inflation should also fall if economic agents believe the government is sincere in its efforts to end inflation (i.e., that the government will not reverse its policy in the face of rising unemployment). As inflation expectations fall so will wage demands, and falling wage demands will bring about a lower unemployment rate (since employers will have more demand for labor when labor costs fall). Ultimately, the economy will move back to full employment at a zero inflation rate or a stable price level. Thus, the important steps in the sequence are (1) a convincing government policy to reduce the inflation rate to zero; (2) toleration of an above normal rate of unemployment; and (3) the adjustment of inflation expectations and wage demands to the lower rate of inflation. In practice, policymakers have shown a preference for stimulating the economy before inflation hits zero, so that unemployment returns to the full employment rate faster. As a result, most recessions have featured a falling but still positive inflation rate.

## Inflation and Expectations

Economists believe that expectations of future inflation play an important role in the relationship between inflation and unemployment. To illustrate why, consider the example of tightening monetary policy (raising short-term interest rates) to reduce the inflation rate. Higher interest rates reduce spending on interest-sensitive goods, such as business investment spending, consumer durables, and housing. As spending on these goods declines, so will employment in the sectors producing these goods. If inflation expectations are low, the overall decline in spending and employment will put downward pressure on prices, as discussed in the previous section. But if inflation expectations are high, prices will respond less quickly to the same decline in spending and employment. As a result, spending and employment would have to fall further and longer to produce the same decline in prices. Whether inflation expectations are high or low will depend importantly on the perceived credibility of the Fed's commitment to maintaining low inflation. If businesses and workers do not believe that the Fed will stick with a policy of tighter monetary policy when faced with higher unemployment, they may not be willing to lower their price demands and wage demands, respectively.

## THE ECONOMIC COSTS OF INFLATION

Economists often discuss jointly the costs to an economy from unemployment and inflation because, for much of the period since the late 1950s, it was generally believed that a long-run tradeoff existed between the two.[10] While the cost of unemployment was well articulated, the cost of inflation was relegated to "shoe leather."[11]

The high U.S. inflation rate of the late 1960s, 1970s, and early 1980s caused economists to rethink the costs of inflation to an economy. What follows is a distillation of those efforts.

Describing the costs to an economy from inflation can be confusing for several reasons. First and foremost there is the confusion over the cost to the economy versus the cost to specific individuals. Costs to individuals may not impose a burden on the economy because they are in the nature of a redistribution of either income and/or wealth. What is lost by some is gained by others. Nevertheless, some of these redistributions can have real effects.

Second, some of the costs of inflation are permanent in the sense that so long as the inflation continues the costs will be incurred. Others are only transitory and arise as the economy moves from one inflation rate to another or because the rate of inflation itself is variable.

Third, some costs are incurred only because the inflation is unanticipated while other costs arise even when the inflation is fully anticipated. Finally, some costs occur only because of the absence for one reason or another of appropriate safeguards: for example, the absence of indexed contracts.

## INFLATION COSTS IN A FULLY INDEXED ECONOMY

As an introduction to understanding the costs imposed on an economy by inflation, consider first an economy that is completely indexed for inflation. Thus every conceivable contract is adjusted for changes in the price level including those for debt (bonds and mortgages) and wages and salaries; where taxes are imposed only on real returns to assets, where tax brackets, fines and all payments imposed by law are indexed, where the exchange rate is free to vary and there are no legal restrictions imposed on interest rates, etc.

In this economy, the distinction between anticipated and unanticipated inflation is unimportant except if the inflation rate is high and the indexed adjustments are not continuous. Then real costs can occur. However, for analytical purposes, assume that all individuals perfectly anticipated the inflation and that the indexed adjustments are continuous.

In this economy, inflation can impose only two real costs: the less efficient arrangement of transactions that result from holding smaller money balances and the necessity to change posted prices more frequently (the so-called menu costs).

The first of these, entailing the rearrangement of transactions due to the higher costs of holding money, is the one cost uniformly identified in the text books as "the cost of inflation." It is worth considering what is involved.

Both individuals and businesses hold money balances because it allows each to arrange transactions in an optimum or least cost way (e.g., for business this involves paying employees, holding inventories, billing customers, maintaining working balances, etc.) and to provide security against an uncertain future. Holding wealth or assets in a money form, however, is not costless. A measure of the so-called opportunity cost is the expected rate of inflation, a cost that rises because wealth can be held in alternative forms whose price or value rises with inflation.

When inflation occurs or when the rate of inflation rises, holding money becomes more costly. Individuals and businesses then attempt to get by with less money (for businesses this may mean billing customers more frequently, paying employees more frequently, etc.). This means that least cost transactions patterns are no longer least cost. The new patterns are less efficient—they use more time or more resources to effect a given transaction. In addition, holding smaller real money balances also reduces the security money provides against an uncertain future.

The magnitude of this cost has been reduced in the United States in recent years because financial institutions can now pay interest on a variety of deposits that function as money. Thus, the primary cost of inflation on money holding applies to currency on which no interest is paid. To the extent, however, that financial institutions are slow to raise interest rates in tandem with inflation, deposit holders will economize on holding deposits and arrange transactions less efficiently, thereby imposing a short-run cost on the economy.

The other cost imposed by inflation in a fully indexed economy is the so-called menu cost, which involves the extra time and resources that are used in adjusting prices more frequently in an environment where prices are rising. These additional costs are incurred mainly with goods and services that are sold in nonauction markets. It does not apply to auction markets where prices change more or less continuously in response to shifts in supply and demand.

## Inflation Costs in a Partially Indexed Economy

### Inflation Anticipated

Very few economies are fully indexed, even those in which inflation is severe. In the United States, indexation is incomplete. As such, inflation can impose costs even if it is fully anticipated. A case in point involves the arrangements for levying taxes. Taxes are levied in several instances on nominal as opposed to real income. As a result, the interaction of inflation and taxation can impose real effects on an economy by altering the incentives to work, save, and invest. Several examples should suffice to explain what is involved.

First, consider an individual who, in a non-inflationary period, earns a real rate of interest of 5% and who pays taxes of 30% on this income. The aftertax real rate of interest is 3.5%, that is, [5% –(30% × 5%)]. Now, assume that a 10% rate of inflation is expected over the one-year term of the loan. As a result, the market rate of interest rises to 15% (composed of a real rate of 5% and an expected inflation rate of 10%). At a tax rate of 30%, the aftertax rate of return falls to 0.5%.[12] To the extent that saving is responsive to the real aftertax rate of return, taxing nominal yields, as is done in the United States, distorts the incentive for individuals to save.[13] (The existing empirical evidence for the United States suggests that private sector saving is quite insensitive to the aftertax rate of return.)

Second, consider what happens to the real aftertax rate of return on business capital during an inflation. For tax purposes, the depreciation of business plant and equipment is based on actual or historic costs. During an inflation, charging depreciation based on historic cost raises the nominal profits of businesses and the basis on which corporate profits taxes are levied. As a result, the aftertax real rate of return falls and this discourages businesses from adding to their stock of plant, equipment, and structures—the bases for future economic growth.14 [15]

Third, to the extent that income tax brackets are not indexed or not indexed completely, inflation in a progressive income tax system can reduce the real aftertax income for wage and salary earners over time, distorting the incentives to work.

During the 1980s, the U.S. tax code was rewritten to adjust the tax brackets for inflation as well as to reduce the level and progressivity of the federal income tax. As a result, inflation has a much reduced interaction with federal taxes in reducing aftertax real income.

Several private sector practices also interact with inflation to produce real economic effects. The first is the continuation of level payment nominal mortgages for financing housing. This practice front loads the real cost of a mortgage during an inflation and, as a result, it discourages the purchase of homes, especially by younger first-time buyers.

Second, business firms continue to record all data in terms of the dollar even though the real purchasing power of this important unit of measure varies considerably over time. This practice has the potential for distorting the real profitability of business over time as well as the valuation of other relevant magnitudes. Since these nominal magnitudes are frequently used as the basis for borrowing and lending decisions, they have the potential for seriously distorting resource allocations.[16]

## Inflation Unanticipated

In this section, the real effects of inflation are analyzed in an environment where it is unanticipated and where the economy relies on nominal or unindexed contracts. In this situation, an important effect of inflation is to redistribute both income and wealth. It would be a mistake, however, to conclude that because gainers and losers cancel, there can be no real effects from inflation.

To see one such real effect, consider what happens to the interest bearing public debt. Inflation reduces the real value of the public debt and with it the real value of the wealth of the private sector, the ultimate owners of most of that debt. Thus, inflation redistributes wealth from the private to the public sector. But who constitutes the public sector? These are the taxpayers who also happen to be the members of the private sector, some of whom own the debt.

Thus, redistribution reduces the real value of the taxes needed to service this debt, and the reduction is most beneficial for the younger workers in the current population and for future generations. As a result of the fall in real tax burden, their real disposable income rises, both today and in the future.

They are thus able to save more while older workers and retirees will, no doubt, have to reduce their consumption, for while they are faced with a large wealth loss, they gain very little from the reduced tax burden. Thus, the redistribution of wealth between the private and the public sectors is really a redistribution between generations that could have an effect on the rate of capital formation.

Perhaps the most serious effect of unanticipated inflation in a market economy is its potential to make the price system malfunction and misallocate resources. Those who live in market economies are apt to take its functioning for granted. They may fail to appreciate or understand the vital role that prices perform in such a system. As standard textbooks in economics teach, the price system determines what is produced, how it is produced, and to whom the output is distributed.

For the price system to perform these functions efficiently, producers must be able to discern a change in real or relative prices from a change in nominal prices which essentially leaves all relative prices unchanged. Only with the former will it be profitable to alter production. A similar phenomenon holds for workers. A rise in money wages may bring forth a greater quantity of labor time if workers are convinced that this is a rise in real wages, that is, money wages relative to prices.[17]

It is easier for producers and workers to discern these changes in real prices and wages if the price level is stable or if the inflation rate is constant. It is more difficult when the rate of inflation is rising and/or more variable. Under these circumstances market economies are apt to have "signal" problems.

That is, producers and workers mistake changes in nominal prices and wages for changes in corresponding real magnitudes and act accordingly. The resulting changes in output and labor time are inefficient and would not have occurred but for the mistakes in perception. Some economists, including Fed

Chairman Ben Bernanke, have argued that low and stable inflation is conducive to higher long-term economic growth.[18] A "signal extraction" problem may not have arisen in the United States, however, since rates of inflation have been relatively low and stable.

## INFLATION AND UNCERTAINTY

Empirical studies completed in the 1970s support the view that inflation is associated with greater uncertainty about future prices and that the degree of uncertainty rises with the rate of inflation.[19]

Rising uncertainty about future prices is believed to produce several possible "real" effects. First, individuals appear to shift from buying assets denominated in nominal terms (e.g., bonds) to so-called real assets such as residential structures, land, precious metals, art work, etc. Because some of these assets are in fairly fixed supply, the resulting capital gain produced by the shift could conceivably raise private sector wealth by a sufficient amount to cause a fall in the saving rate. Second, to compensate for the perceived greater uncertainty, lenders appear to require a greater real reward for supplying funds for investment. Third, contracts tend to be shortened.

The first two developments lead to rising real interest rates, which tend to reduce the rate of investment and capital formation. The third development leads businessmen to prefer shorter lived assets.

## CAN A LITTLE INFLATION "GREASE THE WHEELS" OF THE ECONOMY?

A few prominent economists have broken with the mainstream view that inflation should be kept to a minimum. They have argued that moderate rates of inflation, in the 3%-5% range rather than the 1%-3% range, might be useful for smoother economic adjustment.[20] In a downturn, economic output falls because of "price stickiness"—prices and wages cannot adjust quickly enough to maintain full employment, so total spending falls below the productive capacity of the economy. These economists argue that with a higher average rate of inflation, adjustment would happen more quickly because real wage or price cuts would be possible while avoiding nominal wage cuts. For example, a worker might resist a 2% nominal cut in his wages when inflation is zero, but accept a 3% nominal wage increase when inflation is 5%. In both cases, real wages would have adjusted downward by 2%, but the latter example would have possibly occurred more quickly. Inherent in this view is that individuals suffer from some "money illusion" at moderate rates of inflation (i.e., a 2% real wage cut is accepted because the 3% nominal increase is not seen as a cut.) The existence of "money illusion" is inconsistent with anticipated inflation, and is only possible if inflation is insignificant; there is significant evidence that individuals in high inflation economies are highly sensitive to the inflation rate.[21]

Another argument made for targeting a higher (but still moderate) inflation rate is that deflation (falling prices) is a more serious problem than inflation, with Japan as an example of a country stuck in a long period of deflation and sluggish economic growth. A higher average inflation rate makes it less likely that a country would slide into deflation during a downturn. The reason that it could be hard to escape deflation is related to the "zero bound" on monetary policy.[22] The Federal Reserve can only reduce short-term interest rates to zero when it is stimulating the economy, but sometimes, as was the case in 2008, further stimulus is needed to end a recession. With a higher average rate of inflation, average interest rates would also be expected to be higher. Higher average interest rates would be further from the zero bound on average, so that the Federal Reserve could undertake more stimulus before hitting the zero bound. This argument neglects the fact that the Fed can undertake (and has recently undertaken[23]) unconventional monetary policy actions and expansionary fiscal policy to further stimulate the economy at the zero bound.

## Economic Costs of Inflation: Summary

What is the cost of inflation? It is customary in textbooks to answer this question in terms of a situation where the rate of inflation is anticipated by all market participants who can either continuously re-contract or in which everyone is protected from inflation through indexation. In this world the cost to an economy from inflation is the increased resource cost from conducting transactions with reduced holdings of money—popularly termed "shoe leather" costs. If the inflation is serious, this cost is by no means trivial.[24]

However, inflations are seldom perfectly anticipated. In this situation, perhaps the most serious real effect comes from the ability of rising prices to jam the price signals that are so important to the smooth and efficient functioning of a market economy. Evidence suggests that this may not have been a problem for the United States in the post-World War II era.

In general, the cost of inflation to an economy will be larger the higher the rate of inflation, the more variable the rate, the less it is anticipated, the greater is the uncertainty it causes, and the less indexed is the economy.

# THE MEASUREMENT OF INFLATION

## Changes in the Prices of Goods and Services

There is no single measurement of inflation. The rise in the general level of prices, the essence of inflation, is measured by using a price index that aggregates the price of different goods and services. Ideally, the price index used should be broad based and one in which the individual prices are weighted to indicate their importance to the economy. Many different price indexes are available in the United States that measure different types of inflation rates.

For purposes of this report, two separate price indexes are used. The first is very broad based and derived from the measurement of the nation's gross domestic product (GDP), covering price changes of consumption, investment, government, and traded goods. The other is the Consumer Price Index (CPI), which prices a "market basket" of goods and services purchased by an urban family, a market basket whose individual items are weighted by how much the urban family spent on them in a base year period—currently 1982-1984. Inflation rates according to the two measures are usually similar. Inflation, according to the CPI, was very low (usually below 2%) in the 1950s and early 1960s, began rising in the late 1960s, was relatively high in the 1970s and early 1980s (rising above 10% in 1974 and 1979-1981), began falling in the mid-1980s, and generally remained in the 2%-3% range in the 1990s and 2000s. [25] Inflation tends to rise over the course of an economic expansion and decline during an economic recession, for reasons discussed above (see "The Relationship Between Inflation and Unemployment").

Current CPI data can be accessed at http://www.bls.gov/news. release/pdf/cpi.pdf.

Current data for the GDP price deflator can be accessed at http://www. bea.gov/newsreleases/ national/gdp/gdpnewsrelease.htm.

## THE UNDERLYING OR CORE RATE OF INFLATION

When comparing purchasing power over two time periods, the overall (referred to as "headline") inflation rate is the relevant measure. Comparisons over time of wages, wealth, rates of return, government transfers such as Social Security payments, and so on should all use a headline measure of inflation, because all of these concepts depend on a broad measure of inflation. Although the headline rate of inflation can provide much useful information to policymakers on the state of the economy, it can also be misleading since it responds to both systematic and random forces. The latter can best be understood by reference to the food component of the CPI. An unusual cold spell in Florida in January that damages a substantial part of the fresh produce crop can send food prices and the CPI soaring. A similar effect can be produced by an unusually wet summer in the Midwest. Alternatively, an unusually good combination of rain and sunshine can produce a bountiful harvest and lower prices. Energy prices are also susceptible to such random effects associated with events such as turmoil in major oil producing nations.

To minimize the confusing signals that could arise from the use of the actual rate of inflation, some economists prefer to use a price index that reflects basically only systematic forces to measure inflation. For some economists, this can be achieved by using the CPI less its food and energy components. (It should be noted that food and energy represent about 25% of the current CPI.) Others want to use a moving average either of the CPI itself or of the current CPI less its food and energy components. The use of a moving average is based on the belief that if there are random factors that influence the actual inflation rate, they have an average value of zero. Hence, the use of a moving average should minimize their influence. Others prefer a more complicated measure that trims off whatever prices have changed most in that period.[26]

Policymakers, particularly at the Federal Reserve, often refer to core inflation in their policy decisions. Some policymakers prefer to use core inflation to predict future overall inflation because food and energy price volatility makes it difficult to discern trends from the overall inflation rate. A drawback of an over-reliance on core inflation, however, is that an extended period of rapidly rising food or energy prices could cause all other prices to accelerate. A focus on core may cause policymakers to fail to react to such a rise in inflation until it is too late. This scenario may have occurred in the last decade. Since CPI less food and energy was higher than headline CPI in each year of the decade except 2002 and 2009, a focus on core inflation may have led policymakers to wait too long to tighten policy in the expansion. Furthermore, several studies have failed to find core inflation to be a good forecaster of future inflation, casting doubt on the very rationale for relying on it. [27]

Current data for the CPI less food and energy can be accessed at http://www.bls.gov/news.release/ pdf/cpi.pdf.

### Changes in Labor Costs

Because labor costs comprise nearly two-thirds of the value of final output, some economists believe that they are an important determinant of the rate of inflation. However, changes in the rate of growth of labor costs must be read with care. Wage increases can be driven by productivity increases, tight labor markets, inflation, or fears of inflation. One way to determine the force or forces driving wage increases is to examine what happens to per-unit labor costs. To this end, two major measures of labor cost are available, a comprehensive measure of wage and benefit costs, the *employment cost index,* and *per-unit labor costs in the nonfarm business sector*.

The growth rate of both measures of labor cost generally showed a tendency to accelerate during the expansions of the 1980s and 1990s as labor markets tightened. Subsequent recessions and growing unemployment had a depressing effect on the rise in both measures. During the expansion beginning in 2002, the rate of increase in both measures was fairly comparable to the inflation rate (meaning real wage growth was low) even as the unemployment rate fell.

Current data for the employment cost index can be accessed at http://www.bls.gov/news.release/ pdf/eci.pdf.

Current data for per unit labor costs can be accessed at http://www.bls.gov/news.release/pdf/ prod2.pdf.

## Conclusion

Inflation can impose a real cost on society in terms of the efficiency with which the exchange mechanism works, by distorting the incentives to save, invest, and work, and by providing incorrect signals that needlessly alter production and work effort. Because of this, policymakers should be concerned with the ongoing rate of inflation and any tendency for it to accelerate. An additional reason for concern arises because efforts to reduce the rate of inflation have often been associated with economic downturns. It should not be forgotten that the double-digit inflation of the early 1980s was reduced only through an economic downturn during which the unemployment rate rose to its highest level since the Great Depression of the 1930s. It is argued that the tendency for the inflation rate to accelerate in the late 1980s was a major reason why the Federal Reserve tightened monetary policy, which was also an important factor causing the recession of 1990-1991. Inflationary developments subsequent to that recession have been encouraging. The inflation rate has shown either no or only a modest tendency to rise as unemployment came down. Using various measures, the inflation rate since 1993 was low by standards of the preceding decade. Nonetheless, inflation has risen modestly preceding the 2001 and 2009 recessions, illustrating that this is still an important measure to watch for evaluating the state of the economy. Given the relationship between inflation and the money supply, some economists are concerned that the rapid growth in the portion of the money supply controlled by the Fed from 2008-2011 could cause rapid inflation. To date, those concerns have not been realized, primarily because of the large slack in the economy.

## End Notes

[1] In this and the following paragraph, all changes in the price level are as measured by the Consumer Price Index.

[2] Especially troublesome for the definition of inflation is how to define a rise in the price of an important commodity such as oil. Since it enters as an important input into the production process as well as being a final product, it may cause many other individual prices to rise. Is this a rise in relative prices or is it more appropriately defined as inflation? Economists differ on how to describe this phenomenon. Some blame OPEC for the inflation of the 1970s and early 1980s. Others treat this as a rise in relative prices and attribute the inflation of the period to misplaced policies of the Federal Reserve.

[3] The words "somewhat substantial" cannot be defined precisely. All of the major price indexes have a number of shortcomings, such as only imperfectly correcting for changes in the quality of the goods and services contained in the index. For that reason, relatively low rates for inflation (e.g., plus or minus 2% or less) are often taken to be equivalent to price level stability.

[4] Perhaps the only exception to this statement is the inflation during the Korean War of 1950-1953.

[5] Milton Friedman, *What Price Guideposts in Guidelines: Formal Controls of the Marketplace*, Aliber, Robert and George Schultz, ed. (University of Chicago Press, 1966), p. 18.

[6] For more information, see CRS Report RL30354, *Monetary Policy and the Federal Reserve: Current Policy and Conditions*, by Marc Labonte and Joseph R. McCormack.

[7] For more information, see CRS Report R41540, *Quantitative Easing and the Growth in the Federal Reserve's Balance Sheet*, by Marc Labonte.

[8] This view is commonly held by economists associated with the late Nicholas Kaldor and systematically explained by him in "Monetarism and U.K. Monetary Policy," *Cambridge Journal of Economics*, vol. 4 (1980), pp. 293-318.

[9] For more information, see CRS Report RL30391, *Inflation and Unemployment: What is the Connection?*, by Brian W. Cashell.

[10] A comprehensive discussion of the costs of inflation can be found in Fischer, Stanley, and Franco Modigliani, "Towards an Understanding of the Real Effects and Costs of Inflation," *Weltwirtschaftliches Archiv*, vol. 114, no. 4 (1978), pp. 736-787.

[11] Before financial institutions could pay explicit interest on deposits that function as money, economists believed that individuals and businesses would shift their wealth into savings-type deposits on which interest was paid. Because of this, they would have to make more frequent trips to banks to obtain money. This involved primarily a cost of shoe leather, as shoes wore out more frequently because of the increased number of trips. Hence the often expressed view that the primary cost of inflation to an economy was "shoe leather." More generally, it refers to the resources devoted to avoiding anticipated inflation.

[12] The after-tax real rate is equal to: 15% - 4.5% (which is 30% of 15%) = after-tax nominal yield of 10.5% - 10.0% inflation = 0.5% real after-tax yield.

[13] The possibility arises that the interaction of inflation and the taxation of nominal rates of return will produce negative aftertax real rates of return.

[14] The taxation of nominal profits may also encourage business to opt for shorter-lived capital during an inflation. In addition, since interest expenses are deductible for tax purposes, inflation encourages businesses to finance expansion by the use of debt as opposed to equity. This can impart an element of instability to the financial structure of the economy.

[15] Inflation can also influence some public decision-making because it leads to a misrepresentation of the reported statistics on which these decisions are made. Specifically, the Federal budget deficit tends to be overstated because the inflation premium in interest rates that represents the repayment of principal, is reported as interest expense in both the federal budget accounts and the GNP accounts. To the extent that public concern centers on the current operating outlays of the federal government, true interest outlays are considerably less than currently reported in the budget and, thus, the current operating deficit is much smaller than reported in the federal budget document.

[16] These distortions could be minimized if the dollar was defined as a real unit of account (e.g., defined in terms of a standard basket of commodities). Several proposals for doing so have been put forth. See Warren L. Coats, Jr., *In Search of Monetary Anchor: A "New" Monetary Standard*, IMF Working Paper, 1989.

[17] The key word in this explanation is "may," for a rise in real wages has both a substitution and an income effect. The substitution effect will cause workers to substitute work for leisure while the rise in real income will make leisure a more attractive option to working. Whether the quantity of labor time increases or decreases as the real wage rises will depend on which effect is stronger.

[18] Ben Bernanke Testimony Before the Committee on Banking, Housing, and Urban Affairs, U.S. Senate November 15, 2005.

[19] There are numerous studies that provide support for this view. Some are cited in the references in the Fischer and Modigliani study on which this section is based.

[20] See, for example, George A. Akerlof, William T. Dickens, George L. Perry, *The Macroeconomics of Low Inflation*, Brookings Papers on Economic Activity, Vol. 1996, No.

1 (1996), pp. 1-76. Laurence Ball, *Testimony Before the House Committee on Financial Services,* March 25, 2010.

[21] While proponents of a higher but still moderate inflation target would not deny that there would be higher "shoe leather" costs associated with such a proposal, they would argue that the higher costs would not be great enough to outweigh the benefits.

[22] See, for example, Olivier Blanchard et al., "Rethinking Macroeconomic Policy," International Monetary Fund, *Staff Position Note 10/3*, February 2010.

[23] For more information on recent unconventional monetary actions, see CRS Report RL34427, *Financial Turmoil: Federal Reserve Policy Responses*, by Marc Labonte.

[24] It should be noted that this is not a one-time cost. The costs will be incurred as long as the inflation continues.

[25] Given that the CPI imperfectly measures the "true" rate of inflation, a stable price level or a "true" zero rate of inflation is thought to prevail when the inflation rate as measured by the CPI falls within a range of from 0.5% to 2.0%—this being the possible range of error in the current CPI.

[26] Economists have tried to find the best measure of core inflation according to different criteria. See Timothy Cogley, "A Simple Adaptive Measure of Core Inflation," *Journal of Money, Credit and Banking,* vol. 34, no. 1, February 2002, pp. 94-113; Danny Quah and Shaun P. Vahey, "Measuring Core Inflation," *The Economic Journal,* vol. 105, no. 432, September 1995, pp. 1130-1144; Michael Bryan and Stephen Cecchetti, "Measuring Core Inflation," in N. Gregory Mankiw, ed., *Monetary Policy*, (Chicago: University of Chicago Press, 1994), p. 195; Todd Clark, "Comparing Measures of Core Inflation," Federal Reserve Bank of Kansas City, *Economic Review*, 2002:2, p. 5.

[27] See Robert Rich and Charles Steindel, "A Review of Core Inflation and an Evaluation of Its Measures," Federal Reserve Bank of New York, staff report no. 236, December 2005. This study examines the forecasting power of inflation less food and energy, as well as alternative definitions of core inflation that have been proposed by others, and found that "no core measure does an outstanding job forecasting [headline] CPI inflation ... we find no strong evidence to suggest that a selected core measure will be able to retain its usefulness as a tool to forecast inflation for any given period...." Todd Clark, "Comparing Measures of Core Inflation," Federal Reserve Bank of Kansas City, *Economic Review*, 2002:2, p. 5. This study did not find a statistically significant relationship between core inflation and future headline inflation, although the relationship becomes significant when limited to a more recent time period. Michael Bryan and Stephen Cecchetti, "Measuring Core Inflation," in N. Gregory Mankiw, ed., *Monetary Policy* (Chicago: University of Chicago Press, 1994), p. 195; and Julie Smith, "Weighted Median Inflation: Is This Core Inflation?" *Journal of Money, Credit, and Banking*, April 2004, vol. 36, no. 2, p. 253. Both of these studies compared the forecasting ability of many measures of inflation, and concluded that headline inflation is a better predictor of future headline inflation than core inflation and weighted median measure of inflation performed best. Frederic Mishkin, "Headline versus Core Inflation in the Conduct of Monetary Policy," speech at the Business Cycles, International Transmission and Macroeconomic Policies Conference, Montreal, Canada, October 20, 2007. This study used the Fed's macro model of the U.S. economy to show that when the Fed reacts to changes in headline inflation instead of core inflation, future inflation will be slightly less volatile, but unemployment will be significantly more volatile.

In: Inflation and the Consumer Price Index ISBN: 978-1-61942-705-1
Editors: E. L. Green, A. N. Walker 

*Chapter 2*

# THE CONSUMER PRICE INDEX: A BRIEF OVERVIEW*

***Brian W. Cashell***

## SUMMARY

The Consumer Price Index (CPI) is perhaps the most widely reported measure of inflation. A number of federal government programs are regularly adjusted to account for changes in the CPI, such as Social Security benefits and the personal income tax rate schedule. Thus, the behavior of the CPI has important consequences for a large number of people. Many, however, may be unfamiliar with how the CPI is estimated.

For Congress, the CPI is of particular interest because of its significant effect on the federal budget. Changes in the CPI can have substantial effects on both revenues and outlays, and those changes may either reflect underlying economic conditions or result from methodological changes in the way the CPI is calculated.

The CPI is based on a number of sample surveys. One of these surveys estimates the purchasing patterns of the "typical" household to determine how that household spends its money. Another survey determines where those households shop, and a third survey collects prices on the goods and services purchased by those households.

---

* This is an edited, reformatted and augmented version of a Congressional Research Service publication, CRS Report for Congress RL30074, from www.crs.gov, dated February 17, 2010.

The CPI measures the price level relative to a particular period. Currently, the CPI number for each month is a measure of the price level relative to what it was between 1982 and 1984. The CPI is available for a number of metropolitan areas but it does not allow comparisons of the cost of living in different cities.

## INTRODUCTION

The Consumer Price Index (CPI) is probably the most widely used measure of inflation. A number of federal government programs, such as Social Security benefits and civil service retirement, are tied to increases in the CPI. In addition, the personal income tax rate schedule is indexed to the CPI.[1] Economists use the CPI to calculate constant-dollar estimates of other economic indicators, such as retail sales and hourly earnings, which allow analysis of changes in these variables excluding the effect of changes in the price level. Each year, the CPI is used to update the income levels that determine the poverty rate. Periodic increases in many union wage and other contracts are also tied to increases in the CPI. Thus, the behavior of the CPI has major consequences for a significant portion of the population; but many may be unfamiliar with the details of its calculation.

## BACKGROUND

The CPI is published by the Department of Labor's Bureau of Labor Statistics (BLS).[2] There is no specific legislation authorizing or requiring BLS to calculate and publish the CPI. Neither has legislation ever been enacted to require BLS to adopt any particular methodology in calculating the CPI. When the Bureau of Labor was first created in 1888, its task was, among other duties, to "acquire and diffuse among the people of the United States useful information on subjects connected with labor, in the most general and comprehensive sense of the word.... "[3]

In 1913, the Bureau of Labor was transferred to the newly created Department of Labor and renamed the Bureau of Labor Statistics. BLS was given slightly more specific instructions:

> The Bureau of Labor Statistics, under the direction of the Secretary of Labor, shall collect, collate, and report at least once each year, or oftener if

> necessary, full and complete statistics of the conditions of labor and the products and distribution of the products of the same ... and said Secretary of Labor may collate, arrange, and publish such statistical information so obtained in such manner as to him may seem wise.[4]

Two CPIs are published by the BLS, the Consumer Price Index for Urban Wage Earners and Clerical Workers (CPI-W), and the Consumer Price Index for All Urban Consumers (CPI-U). The CPI-W is based on the purchasing patterns of only those in the population who earn more than half of their income from clerical or wage occupations, and were employed at least 37 weeks in the previous year.5 The CPI-W population makes up about 32% of the total population. Prior to 1978, the CPI-W was the only CPI published. Beginning in 1978, the CPI-U was introduced so that a broader share of the population would be represented in estimates of changes in the price level. The CPI-U is based on the expenditure patterns of all urban consumers and covers about 87% of the population. The CPI-U is usually the more publicized of the two price indexes.

Although the CPI-U and CPI-W are slightly different indexes, the numerical difference between the two measures is typically small. Between 1989 and 2009, the CPI-U increased, overall, by 73.0% compared with an increase of 71.0% for the CPI-W. Over the same period, that translates into an average annual rate of change of 2.8% for the CPI-U and 2.7% for the CPI-W.

Both the CPI-W and the CPI-U are used for inflation indexing by the federal government.[6] One advantage to using the CPI in indexing is that the CPI is rarely revised.[7] Definitions, the index base year, the goods and services accounted for, and the methodology used to calculate the CPI may change from time to time, but, once published, the actual index number is final.[8] Using other measures of the price level, such as one of the price indexes associated with Gross Domestic Product, for indexing purposes poses the problem of which number to use, the preliminary estimate or one of many subsequent revisions.[9]

Since the release of January 2007 data, the CPI and all of its component indexes have been published rounded to three decimal places rather than one. The change was not meant to imply any increase in the accuracy of the CPI. Instead it is being done to maintain precision in published estimates of percentage changes. Prior to 2007, when BLS published the CPI rounded to only one decimal place, it based published figures of percentage change in the CPI on those rounded numbers so that they could be replicated by users of published CPI data. But doing that meant that some precision in the published percent change data was lost.[10] The effect of the change was expected to be small.[11]

## Estimating the CPI

Both CPIs are based on retail market prices. These prices, for more than 80,000 separate items, are collected in 87 urban areas across the country from thousands of outlets, such as grocery and department stores, gasoline service stations, and hospitals, among others.[12] BLS selects these retail establishments based on a survey showing where people do their shopping. Actual prices (except those for food) are not published because they are collected on a confidential basis.

Price indexes are available in considerable detail. Examples of items for which CPI data are available include white bread, men's shirts, automobile tires, haircuts, funerals, automobile repair, and bedroom furniture.

The "all-items" CPI is the index most often referred to and it is a composite index, a weighted average, based on the indexes for all of the goods and services whose prices are collected.

The all-items CPI measures the price change of a fixed market basket of goods and services over time. The mix of goods and services making up the market basket is based on spending patterns established by the Consumer Expenditure Survey (CES).[13] Based on the CES, weights are assigned to each of the goods and services that make up the market basket. These weights determine how much the price change for a given good will affect the all-items measure.

For any given interval, the total price change, as measured by the all-items CPI, is the weighted average of the price changes of all of the components. With the release of data for January 2010, the CPI market basket is based on purchasing patterns described by the CES in 2007 and 2008. BLS updates the expenditure weights every two years.

*Table 1* shows the major expenditure categories included in the CPI and their relative importance in the CPI-U as of December 2009. Relative importance reflects both the expenditure weights and changes in relative prices. Either a larger expenditure weight, or an increase in the price of a good relative to prices for other goods may cause the relative importance to increase, and vice versa.

**Table 1. Expenditure Categories and Relative Importance in the CPI-U**

| Expenditure Category | Relative Importance, December 2009 |
|---|---|
| All items | 100.000 |
| Food and beverages | 14.795 |
| Housing – shelter | 32.289 |
| Housing – fuels and utilities | 5.081 |
| Housing – household furnishings and operation | 4.590 |
| Apparel | 3.695 |
| Transportation | 16.685 |
| Medical care | 6.513 |
| Recreation | 6.437 |
| Education and communication | 6.434 |
| Other goods and services | 3.483 |

Source: Department of Labor, Bureau of Labor Statistics.

## Medical Care

Based on the measures of relative importance shown here, some might be concerned that medical care costs have too small a weight in the all-items index. In particular, the elderly typically spend a relatively larger share of their outlays on medical care. In calculating the CPI, however, the share of the market basket accounted for by medical care is based on "out-of-pocket" costs. This includes direct out-of pocket costs for medical care as well as indirect out-of-pocket costs for health insurance.[14] An increasing share of medical costs are paid for by employers and government, so that out-of-pocket expenses on medical care are not as great as total outlays on medical care.

It is also important to appreciate that there is considerable variation among consumers (and among elderly consumers as well) in the demand for medical care, and the relative importance of medical care in the CPI is based on an average. No single price index can accurately describe the inflation experience of every single person. Different population groups (e.g., the elderly) tend to have different purchasing patterns, and individuals' purchases vary significantly within those groups. Although many elderly may spend more on medical care than is taken into account in the CPI, there are also some elderly who spend less. For those who spend less, if medical care costs rise more rapidly than do the prices of other goods and services, the CPI will tend to overstate increases in the cost of living, other things being equal. BLS is currently investigating the behavior of an experimental CPI for the elderly population.[15] This experimental CPI for Americans aged 62 and older rose by an average of 2.9% per year between December 1989 and December 2009. During the same period, both the CPI-U and CPI-W rose at an annual rate of 2.7%.[16]

Considerable effort is made to ensure that the CPI is a meaningful, reliable measure of changes in the price level. But it does not necessarily reflect the inflation experience of each individual consumer. To the extent that individuals spend relatively more on those goods and services whose prices are rising faster than average, they may experience a higher inflation rate than that measured by the CPI. Similarly, those who spend relatively less on goods and services whose prices are rising faster than average, may experience a lower inflation rate than that measured by the CPI.

If purchasing patterns change significantly, then in the short run the CPI may tend to overstate the inflation rate. The CPI is a fixed-weight index and does not immediately take into account changes in spending patterns due to changes in relative prices. There may also be a tendency for the CPI to overstate the inflation rate because some price increases reflect improvements in the quality of goods and services. Taking quality changes into account in a price index is difficult, but BLS does attempt to make some adjustments to the CPI for quality improvements in a number of areas, including automobiles, apparel, and a number of consumer electronic goods, personal computers in particular.[17]

## Home Ownership

Home ownership costs in the CPI are treated in a special way.[18] Prior to 1983, the home ownership component of the CPI measured changes in the cost of purchasing a new home. Since 1983 for the CPI-U and 1985 for the CPI-W, changes in the cost of home ownership have been based on the concept of "rental equivalence." Rather than measuring changes in the cost of buying a house in each period, which would include finance charges, the CPI attempts to estimate the rental value of owner-occupied housing. Thus, the CPI measures changes in the consumption aspect of housing costs and not changes in the investment value of owner-occupied housing.[19]

## The "Core" CPI

In addition to the all-items CPIs, BLS also publishes an index which excludes the effects of both food and energy prices. Increases in the CPI less food and energy are also referred to as the "core" inflation rate. The reason for excluding food and energy prices is that, at times, they may be more volatile than other prices and thus mask the underlying trend rate of inflation.[20] That can be useful for policymakers to whom inflation is an important variable. The "core" rate is often mentioned prominently in press reports covering the monthly releases of CPI data. This seems to be an occasional source of confusion, leading some to conclude that food and energy prices are not taken into account in calculating Social Security cost-of-living adjustments.[21] In fact, food and energy prices are taken into account. The all-items CPI is used to make cost-of-living adjustments, not the core index.

# Improving the CPI

In December 1996, a special commission chaired by economist Michael Boskin reported to the Senate Finance Committee that the CPI tended to overstate the actual rate of inflation by about 1.1% per year.[22] Although a number of specific recommendations were made in the report, Congress took no legislative steps to require any changes in the way BLS calculates the CPI.[23] But the methodology of calculating the CPI has changed much since it was first published and is likely to continue to do so. BLS continues to look at methods that might lead to a more accurate measure of the cost of living. As part of that process, with the release of data for July 2002, BLS introduced an alternative CPI that makes use of "chain-weights." This index is referred to as the C-CPI-U. The expenditure weights for the C-CPI-U are updated more frequently than either the CPI-U or the CPI-W, and the index itself is subject to revision. The C-CPI-U has not replaced either the CPI-U or the CPI-W, and they will continue to be used for indexing.[24]

# Local Area CPIs

The CPI is currently published for 26 metropolitan areas. For most of these cities, however, indexes are not published on a monthly basis.

**Table 2. Availability of Local Area CPI Data**

| Area | Frequency |
|---|---|
| Northeast Region | monthly |
| Boston-Brockton-Nashua, MA-NH-ME-CT | bimonthly (odd) |
| New York-Northern New Jersey-Long Island, NY-NJ-CT-PA | monthly |
| Philadelphia-Wilmington-Atlantic City. PA-NJ-DE-MD | bimonthly (even) |
| Pittsburgh, PA | semiannually |
| Midwest Region | monthly |
| Chicago-Gary-Kenosha, IL-IN-WI | monthly |
| Cincinnati-Hamilton, OH-KY-IN | semiannually |
| Cleveland-Akron, OH | bimonthly (odd) |
| Detroit-Ann Arbor-Flint, MI | bimonthly (even) |
| Kansas City, MO-KS | semiannually |
| Minneapolis-St. Paul, MN-WI | semiannually |
| Milwaukee-Racine, WI | semiannually |
| St. Louis, MO-IL | semiannually |
| Southern Region | monthly |
| Atlanta, GA | bimonthly (even) |
| Dallas-Fort Worth, TX | bimonthly (odd) |
| Houston-Galveston-Brazoria, TX | bimonthly (even) |
| Miami-Fort Lauderdale, FL | bimonthly (even) |
| Tampa-St. Petersburg-Clearwater, FL | bimonthly (even) |
| Washington-Baltimore, DC-MD-VA-WV | bimonthly (odd) |
| Western Region | monthly |
| Anchorage, AK | semiannually |
| Denver-Boulder-Greeley, CO | semiannually |
| Honolulu, HI | semiannually |
| Los Angeles-Riverside-Orange County, CA | monthly |
| Portland-Salem, OR-WA | semiannually |
| San Diego, CA | semiannually |
| San Francisco-Oakland-San Jose, CA | bimonthly (even) |
| Seattle-Tacoma-Bremerton, WA | bimonthly (even) |

Source: Department of Labor, Bureau of Labor Statistics.

These metropolitan area indexes are only intended to compare inflation *rates* between cities. The metropolitan area CPIs may *not* be used to compare the actual cost of living between cities.[25] *Table 2* shows the metropolitan areas for which the CPI is published as well as the publication frequency.

## CPI Data Via the Internet

BLS has set up an Internet home page for the CPI where visitors can get a copy of the most recent CPI press release, as well as up-to-date information regarding the CPI program. The Internet address for this page is http://www.bls.gov/cpi/.

Detailed CPI data are also readily available. BLS has set up a number of ways on their website, http://www.bls.gov/cpi/#data, to obtain CPI data. By making selections from each of a succession of menus, users of BLS's website may specify the particular data they want. There is also a link to an "inflation calculator," allowing users to make their own inflation adjustments to dollar amounts.

## Historical Data

BLS has published estimates of the CPI going back as far as 1800, which makes it the longest, continuous price index series available. These data are shown in *Table 3*. Data for 1800 through 1912 were derived by splicing price indexes collected in three separate, nongovernmental, studies. Prior to 1978, there was only one CPI available. For 1978 and after, the data in *Table 3* correspond to the CPI-U. Given that the accuracy of the CPI remains a topic of discussion, the data for the early years of this series should be considered to be fairly crude estimates.

The long series allows a noteworthy observation. Between 1800 and 1945, there was no longterm trend in the price level. During that period prices tended to fall as often as they rose. Since 1945, however, there has been a decided upward trend in the level of prices with the price level having fallen in only a few years. The decline in 2009 was the first since 1955.

The figures in *Table 3* show year-over-year changes in the CPI, and the index numbers for each year are the average of the monthly data for that year.

**Table 3. The Consumer Price Index for All Urban Consumers, 1800 – 2009**

| Year | CPI Index (1982-1984 = 100.0) | Percentage Change from Previous Year |
|---|---|---|
| 1800 | 17.0 | |
| 1801 | 16.7 | -2.0 |
| 1802 | 14.3 | -14.0 |
| 1803 | 15.0 | 4.7 |
| 1804 | 15.0 | 0.0 |
| 1805 | 15.0 | 0.0 |
| 1806 | 15.7 | 4.4 |
| 1807 | 14.7 | -6.4 |
| 1808 | 16.0 | 9.1 |
| 1809 | 15.7 | -2.1 |
| 1810 | 15.7 | 0.0 |
| 1811 | 16.7 | 6.4 |
| 1812 | 17.0 | 2.0 |
| 1813 | 19.3 | 13.7 |
| 1814 | 21.0 | 8.6 |
| 1815 | 18.3 | -12.7 |
| 1816 | 17.0 | -7.3 |
| 1817 | 16.0 | -5.9 |
| 1818 | 15.3 | -4.2 |
| 1819 | 15.3 | 0.0 |
| 1820 | 14.0 | -8.7 |
| 1821 | 13.3 | -4.8 |
| 1822 | 13.3 | 0.0 |
| 1823 | 12.0 | -10.0 |
| 1824 | 11.0 | -8.3 |
| 1825 | 11.3 | 3.0 |
| 1826 | 11.3 | 0.0 |
| 1827 | 11.3 | 0.0 |
| 1828 | 11.0 | -2.9 |
| 1829 | 10.7 | -3.0 |
| 1830 | 10.7 | 0.0 |
| 1831 | 10.7 | 0.0 |
| 1832 | 10.0 | -6.3 |
| 1833 | 9.7 | -3.3 |

| Year | CPI Index (1982-1984 = 100.0) | Percentage Change from Previous Year |
|---|---|---|
| 1834 | 10.0 | 3.4 |
| 1835 | 10.3 | 3.3 |
| 1836 | 11.0 | 6.5 |
| 1837 | 11.3 | 3.0 |
| 1838 | 10.7 | -5.9 |
| 1839 | 10.7 | 0.0 |
| 1840 | 10.0 | -6.3 |
| 1841 | 10.3 | 3.3 |
| 1842 | 9.7 | -6.5 |
| 1843 | 9.3 | -3.4 |
| 1844 | 9.3 | 0.0 |
| 1845 | 9.3 | 0.0 |
| 1846 | 9.0 | -3.6 |
| 1847 | 9.3 | 3.7 |
| 1848 | 8.7 | -7.1 |
| 1849 | 8.3 | -3.8 |
| 1850 | 8.3 | 0.0 |
| 1851 | 8.3 | 0.0 |
| 1852 | 8.3 | 0.0 |
| 1853 | 8.3 | 0.0 |
| 1854 | 9.0 | 8.0 |
| 1855 | 9.3 | 3.7 |
| 1856 | 9.0 | -3.6 |
| 1857 | 9.3 | 3.7 |
| 1858 | 8.7 | -7.1 |
| 1859 | 9.0 | 3.8 |
| 1860 | 9.0 | 0.0 |
| 1861 | 9.0 | 0.0 |
| 1862 | 10.0 | 11.1 |
| 1863 | 12.3 | 23.3 |
| 1864 | 15.7 | 27.0 |
| 1865 | 15.3 | -2.1 |
| 1866 | 14.7 | -4.3 |
| 1867 | 14.0 | -4.5 |
| 1868 | 13.3 | -4.8 |
| 1869 | 13.3 | 0.0 |
| 1870 | 12.7 | -5.0 |

**Table 3. (Continued)**

| Year | CPI Index (1982-1984 = 100.0) | Percentage Change from Previous Year |
|---|---|---|
| 1871 | 12.0 | -5.3 |
| 1872 | 12.0 | 0.0 |
| 1873 | 12.0 | 0.0 |
| 1874 | 11.3 | -5.6 |
| 1875 | 11.0 | -2.7 |
| 1876 | 10.7 | -3.0 |
| 1877 | 10.7 | 0.0 |
| 1878 | 9.7 | -9.4 |
| 1879 | 9.3 | -3.4 |
| 1880 | 9.7 | 3.6 |
| 1881 | 9.7 | 0.0 |
| 1882 | 9.7 | 0.0 |
| 1883 | 9.3 | -3.4 |
| 1884 | 9.0 | -3.6 |
| 1885 | 9.0 | 0.0 |
| 1886 | 9.0 | 0.0 |
| 1887 | 9.0 | 0.0 |
| 1888 | 9.0 | 0.0 |
| 1889 | 9.0 | 0.0 |
| 1890 | 9.0 | 0.0 |
| 1891 | 9.0 | 0.0 |
| 1892 | 9.0 | 0.0 |
| 1893 | 9.0 | 0.0 |
| 1894 | 8.7 | -3.7 |
| 1895 | 8.3 | -3.8 |
| 1896 | 8.3 | 0.0 |
| 1897 | 8.3 | 0.0 |
| 1898 | 8.3 | 0.0 |
| 1899 | 8.3 | 0.0 |
| 1900 | 8.3 | 0.0 |
| 1901 | 8.3 | 0.0 |
| 1902 | 8.7 | 4.0 |
| 1903 | 9.0 | 3.8 |
| 1904 | 9.0 | 0.0 |
| 1905 | 9.0 | 0.0 |

| Year | CPI Index (1982-1984 = 100.0) | Percentage Change from Previous Year |
|---|---|---|
| 1906 | 9.0 | 0.0 |
| 1907 | 9.3 | 3.7 |
| 1908 | 9.0 | -3.6 |
| 1909 | 9.0 | 0.0 |
| 1910 | 9.3 | 3.7 |
| 1911 | 9.3 | 0.0 |
| 1912 | 9.7 | 3.6 |
| 1913 | 9.9 | 2.4 |
| 1914 | 10.0 | 1.0 |
| 1915 | 10.1 | 1.0 |
| 1916 | 10.9 | 7.9 |
| 1917 | 12.8 | 17.4 |
| 1918 | 15.1 | 18.0 |
| 1919 | 17.3 | 14.6 |
| 1920 | 20.0 | 15.6 |
| 1921 | 17.9 | -10.5 |
| 1922 | 16.8 | -6.1 |
| 1923 | 17.1 | 1.8 |
| 1924 | 17.1 | 0.0 |
| 1925 | 17.5 | 2.3 |
| 1926 | 17.7 | 1.1 |
| 1927 | 17.4 | -1.7 |
| 1928 | 17.1 | -1.7 |
| 1929 | 17.1 | 0.0 |
| 1930 | 16.7 | -2.3 |
| 1931 | 15.2 | -9.0 |
| 1932 | 13.7 | -9.9 |
| 1933 | 13.0 | -5.1 |
| 1934 | 13.4 | 3.1 |
| 1935 | 13.7 | 2.2 |
| 1936 | 13.9 | 1.5 |
| 1937 | 14.4 | 3.6 |
| 1938 | 14.1 | -2.1 |
| 1939 | 13.9 | -1.4 |
| 1940 | 14.0 | 0.7 |
| 1941 | 14.7 | 5.0 |
| 1942 | 16.3 | 10.9 |

**Table 3. (Continued)**

| Year | CPI Index (1982-1984 = 100.0) | Percentage Change from Previous Year |
|---|---|---|
| 1943 | 17.3 | 6.1 |
| 1944 | 17.6 | 1.7 |
| 1945 | 18.0 | 2.3 |
| 1946 | 19.5 | 8.3 |
| 1947 | 22.3 | 14.4 |
| 1948 | 24.1 | 8.1 |
| 1949 | 23.8 | -1.2 |
| 1950 | 24.1 | 1.3 |
| 1951 | 26.0 | 7.9 |
| 1952 | 26.5 | 1.9 |
| 1953 | 26.7 | 0.8 |
| 1954 | 26.9 | 0.7 |
| 1955 | 26.8 | -0.4 |
| 1956 | 27.2 | 1.5 |
| 1957 | 28.1 | 3.3 |
| 1958 | 28.9 | 2.8 |
| 1959 | 29.1 | 0.7 |
| 1960 | 29.6 | 1.7 |
| 1961 | 29.9 | 1.0 |
| 1962 | 30.2 | 1.0 |
| 1963 | 30.6 | 1.3 |
| 1964 | 31.0 | 1.3 |
| 1965 | 31.5 | 1.6 |
| 1966 | 32.4 | 2.9 |
| 1967 | 33.4 | 3.1 |
| 1968 | 34.8 | 4.2 |
| 1969 | 36.7 | 5.5 |
| 1970 | 38.8 | 5.7 |
| 1971 | 40.5 | 4.4 |
| 1972 | 41.8 | 3.2 |
| 1973 | 44.4 | 6.2 |
| 1974 | 49.3 | 11.0 |
| 1975 | 53.8 | 9.1 |
| 1976 | 56.9 | 5.8 |
| 1977 | 60.6 | 6.5 |

| Year | CPI Index (1982-1984 = 100.0) | Percentage Change from Previous Year |
|---|---|---|
| 1978 | 65.2 | 7.6 |
| 1979 | 72.6 | 11.4 |
| 1980 | 82.4 | 13.5 |
| 1981 | 90.9 | 10.3 |
| 1982 | 96.5 | 6.2 |
| 1983 | 99.6 | 3.2 |
| 1984 | 103.9 | 4.3 |
| 1985 | 107.6 | 3.6 |
| 1986 | 109.6 | 1.9 |
| 1987 | 113.6 | 3.7 |
| 1988 | 118.3 | 4.1 |
| 1989 | 124.0 | 4.8 |
| 1990 | 130.7 | 5.4 |
| 1991 | 136.2 | 4.2 |
| 1992 | 140.3 | 3.0 |
| 1993 | 144.5 | 3.0 |
| 1994 | 148.2 | 2.6 |
| 1995 | 152.4 | 2.8 |
| 1996 | 156.9 | 3.0 |
| 1997 | 160.5 | 2.3 |
| 1998 | 163.0 | 1.6 |
| 1999 | 166.6 | 2.2 |
| 2000 | 172.2 | 3.4 |
| 2001 | 177.1 | 2.8 |
| 2002 | 179.9 | 1.6 |
| 2003 | 184.0 | 2.3 |
| 2004 | 188.9 | 2.7 |
| 2005 | 195.3 | 3.4 |
| 2006 | 201.6 | 3.2 |
| 2007 | 207.342 | 2.8 |
| 2008 | 215.303 | 3.8 |
| 2009 | 214.537 | -0.4 |

Source: Department of Labor, Bureau of Labor Statistics.

Changes in the CPI are sometimes published on a December-over-December basis. That number can vary significantly from the year-over-year number depending on how the monthly changes are distributed over the period. In 2009, for example, the year-over-year change was -0.4% whereas the change from December 2008 to December 2009 was 2.7%.

## CPI Calculations

The CPI is an indicator of changes in the price level. At present, those changes are expressed relative to the average level of prices in the years 1982, 1983, and 1984. Thus, the average of all of the monthly CPI numbers for those three years is equal to 100. Determining the change in consumer prices between any two years is a simple percent change calculation using the formula:

$$\text{percentage change in the CPI} = ((\ CPI2 \div CPI1\ ) - 1\ ) \times 100.$$

For example, in 2009, the CPI-U was 214.537, and in 1989 the CPI-U was 124.0. The total percentage change in the CPI-U between 1989 and 2009 was:

$$((\ 214.537 \div 124.0\ ) - 1\ ) \times 100 = 73.0 \text{ percent.}$$

Calculating the percentage change between any two years at an *annual rate* is slightly more complicated, and requires the formula:

$$\text{annual rate of change in the CPI} = ((\ CPI2 \div CPI1\ )^{1/n} - 1\ ) \times 100,$$

where n is the number of years covered in the interval. To calculate the average annual rate of change in the CPI-U between 1989 and 2009, we use an n of 20 and the same CPI-U values as in the previous example. The average annual rate of change in the CPI-U between 1989 and 2009 was:

$$((\ 214.537 \div 124.0\ )^{1/20} - 1\ ) \times 100 = 2.8 \text{ percent.}$$

Another common use of the CPI is to adjust dollar amounts for inflation, so that amounts from different years can be compared in terms of dollars of the same purchasing power. Suppose the question is how much money would have been required in 2009 to buy the same quantity of goods and services as $100 bought in 1989. To get such an estimate, the 1989 dollar value needs to be adjusted to account for the increase in consumer prices between 1989 and 2009. That requires the formula:

equivalent purchasing power in period 2 = ( CPI2 ÷ CPI1 ) x dollar amount in period 1.

For example, using the same CPI values as in the above examples, the equivalent purchasing power in 2009 of $100 in 1989 is:

( 214.537 ÷ 124.0 ) x $100 = $173.01.

This same calculation can be reversed to find the purchasing power in an earlier period of a dollar amount of a more recent vintage. To do this use the formula:

equivalent purchasing power in period 1 = ( CPI1 ÷ CPI2 ) x dollar amount in period 2.

For example, using the same CPI values as in the above examples, the equivalent purchasing power in 1989 of $100 in 2009 is:

( 124.0 ÷ 214.537 ) x $100 = $57.80.

Using these formulae, dollar values of constant purchasing power can be compared for any two periods for which CPI data are available. Constant dollar values are always compared in terms of the dollar's purchasing power in a particular year, known as the base year. When comparing dollars of constant purchasing power, it is important to specify the base year.

## End Notes

[1] See CRS Report RL34168, Automatic Cost of Living Adjustments: Some Economic and Practical Considerations, by Brian W. Cashell.

[2] BLS began periodic publication of a National CPI in 1921. At first, the CPI was only released semi-annually. Quarterly releases were begun in 1935, and monthly releases began in 1940.

[3] 29 U.S.C. 1.

[4] 29 U.S.C. 2.

[5] Specifically, clerical workers, craft workers, operatives, service workers, or laborers.

[6] The CPI-U is the index used to adjust various provisions of the personal income tax code. The CPI-W is the index used to adjust Social Security benefits.

[7] Historically, BLS has published monthly changes in the CPI on both a seasonally adjusted and not seasonally adjusted basis. The seasonally adjusted changes are subject to revision because seasonal adjustment factors may change over time. BLS also makes available a

seasonally adjusted index number that is subject to revision. Seasonal adjustment does not affect yearly changes because the adjustment factors cancel each other out over any given 12-month period.

[8] An exception to this occurred in 2000. A mathematical error was found in the way the CPI was calculated. As a result, numbers that had already been published were revised.

[9] See U.S. Department of Labor, Bureau of Labor Statistics, Using the Consumer Price Index for Escalation, available at http://www.bls.gov/ cpi/cpi1998d.htm.

[10] See Elliot Williams, "The Effects of Rounding on the Consumer Price Index," Monthly Labor Review, October 2006.

[11] See additional info at the BLS website, at http://www.bls.gov/cpi/ cpithree dec.htm.

[12] See "In the Field With the Price Indexers," New York Times, June 20, 1995, p. D2.

[13] Detailed information on the CES is available on the Internet at http:// www.bls.gov/cex/.

[14] See U.S. Department of Labor, Bureau of Labor Statistics, "Measuring Price Change for Medical Care in the CPI," at http://www.bls.gov/cpi/ cpifact4.htm.

[15] See U.S. Department of Labor, Bureau of Labor Statistics, "Experimental Consumer Price Index for Americans 62 Years of Age and Older, 1998-2003," http://www.bls.gov /cpi/cpiexpcpie2005.pdf.

[16] See CRS Report RS20060, A Separate Consumer Price Index for the Elderly?, by Brian W. Cashell.

[17] See U.S. Department of Labor, Bureau of Labor Statistics, "How BLS Measures Price Change for Personal Computers and Peripheral Equipment in the Consumer Price Index," http://www.bls.gov/cpi/cpifaccomp.htm.

[18] See U.S. Department of Labor, Bureau of Labor Statistics, "Consumer Price Indexes for Rent and Rental Equivalence," at http://www.bls.gov/ cpi/cpifact6.htm.

[19] Because of the timing of this change in the way the CPI is calculated, a permanent upward bias in the level of the CPI was introduced. BLS has published estimates of the CPI-U using the rental equivalence approach for the years 1967 to 1982. This series is known as the CPI-U-X1. The Census Bureau now publishes historical estimates of real money income based on the CPI-U-X1 measure. See U.S. Bureau of the Census, Money Income of Households, Families, and Persons in the United States, Current Population Reports, Series P-60, no.174, 1991, pp. 8-9.

[20] See CRS Report RS22705, Inflation: Core vs. Headline, by Marc Labonte.

[21] John S. Greenlees and Robert McClelland, "Addressing Misconceptions About the Consumer Price Index," Monthly Labor Review, August 2008.

[22] U.S. Congress, Senate Committee on Finance, Final Report of the Advisory Commission to Study the Consumer Price Index, committee print, 104th Cong., 2nd sess., December 1996. For a discussion of methodological changes implemented after the Boskin report, see David S. Johnson, et. al., "Price Measurement in the United States: A Decade After the Boskin Report," Monthly Labor Review, May 2006.

[23] Because of the CPI's budget implications, Congress has, from time to time, taken some interest in how it is calculated. To date, however, no legislation has been enacted that would directly affect BLS' methodology. See David S. Johnson, Stephen B. Reed, and Kenneth J. Stewart, "Price Measurement in the United States: A Decade After the Boskin Report," Monthly Labor Review, May 2006, pp. 10-19.

[24] See CRS Report RL32293, The Chained Consumer Price Index: How Is It Different, and Would It Be Appropriate for Cost-of-Living Adjustments? , by Brian W. Cashell.

[25] The CPI expresses the price level relative to a particular period of time. Currently, the CPI reflects the level of prices relative to the 1982-1984 period. Thus, the average index value

during that period for each metropolitan area will be 100, no matter how expensive any area may be in which to live. That does not mean that each of these metropolitan areas is equally expensive. See CRS Report RS20942, Adjusting Federal Benefits for Geographic Differences in the Cost of Living, by Brian W. Cashell.

In: Inflation and the Consumer Price Index ISBN: 978-1-61942-705-1
Editors: E. L. Green, A. N. Walker 

*Chapter 3*

# INFLATION: CORE VS. HEADLINE*

*Marc Labonte*

## SUMMARY

Inflation measures the rate of change in all prices. Maintaining low and stable inflation is one of the primary goals of macroeconomic policy. But how should inflation be measured? Policymakers, particularly at the Federal Reserve, often refer to *core* inflation in their policy decisions. Core inflation is commonly defined as a measure of inflation that omits changes in food and energy prices. Some policymakers prefer to use core inflation to predict future overall inflation because food and energy price volatility makes it difficult to discern trends from the overall inflation rate. A drawback of an over-reliance on core inflation, however, is that an extended period of rapidly rising food or energy prices could cause all other prices to accelerate. A focus on core may cause policymakers to fail to react to such a rise in inflation until it is too late. This scenario may have occurred recently. Many economists are concerned that rapid increases in food and energy prices are now pushing overall inflation to uncomfortably high levels. Furthermore, several studies have failed to find core inflation to be a good forecaster of future inflation, casting doubt on the very rationale for relying on it.

* This is an edited, reformatted and augmented version of a Congressional Research Service publication, CRS Report for Congress RS22705, from www.crs.gov, dated May 1, 2008.

## INTRODUCTION

Inflation, the general rise in the prices of goods and services, is important to policymakers for several reasons.[1] First, rising inflation is unpopular with the public, in part because some households are more adversely affected by inflation than others. Second, high or rising inflation can reduce productivity by distorting price signals, so that it is hard for businesses to tell if prices are changing in relative terms, and by individuals wasting resources in order to maintain the purchasing power of their wealth. Finally, inflation plays a key role in macroeconomic stabilization policy. Changes in inflation often indicate changes in the business cycle — rising inflation is often a sign that the economy is overheating and falling inflation is a sign that the economy is sluggish. The Federal Reserve (Fed) is mandated to keep inflation low and stable, and alters interest rates in order to do so.[2]

In recent years, the Fed has focused attention on the *core* rate of inflation, a measure of inflation that excludes food and energy prices, in explanations of its policy decisions. For example, in July 2007, the third sentence of the 10-sentence Federal Open Market Committee statement summarizing the committee's policy decision read, "Readings on core inflation have improved modestly in recent months." In Fed Chairman Ben Bernanke's July 2007 testimony to Congress, he stated that "Food and energy prices tend to be quite volatile, so that, looking forward, core inflation...may be a better gauge than overall inflation of underlying inflation trends." When core inflation approached 3% in 2006, Chairman Bernanke said that it had "reached a level that, if sustained, would be at or above the upper end of the range that many economists, including myself, would consider consistent with price stability...."[3] This report defines core inflation, reviews recent trends, and analyzes the advantages and drawbacks of using core inflation.

## DEFINITION

No official measure of "inflation" exists. Inflation is measured as the percent change in a price index. Several indices track price changes, with each data series measuring something different. The most commonly cited measure of inflation is the percent change in the *consumer price index (CPI)*.[4] This index measures the price of a basket of consumer goods and services that is representative of overall consumer purchases in urban areas. When food and energy prices are omitted from the CPI, the remaining basket is commonly referred to as the *core CPI*. The overall measure of CPI, which includes food and energy, is often referred to as the *headline CPI*. Another common measure of inflation is the percent change in the *GDP (gross domestic product) price deflator*, which is used to transform nominal GDP into real GDP. Since the GDP deflator is based on the prices of all goods and services in the economy, it is a broader measure of inflation than the CPI. A subset of the GDP deflator that is conceptually similar to the CPI, but includes more items and areas, is the *personal consumption expenditures (PCE) price deflator*; for technical reasons, the Fed sometimes prefers this measure to the CPI in their analyses. Core measures of the GDP and PCE deflators are also available.

Conceptually, core inflation could be any measure of inflation that attempts to strip out price volatility, but the most common definition of core strips out only two particularly volatile categories of goods, food and energy. The four most volatile items in the CPI are all food or energy products.[5] The standard deviation of energy prices is estimated to be 12 times higher than overall inflation.[6] Omitting food and energy prices from the CPI is not a trivial modification — food and beverages accounted for 15% of the headline CPI basket, and energy accounted for an additional 9% in 2006.

While excluding food from core inflation has become conventional, it may no longer be warranted. The volatility of food has decreased significantly since the 1970s.[7] Until 2007, the recent divergence between headline and core inflation was driven by energy prices. In 2007, food prices rose rapidly — it is too soon to tell whether this development marks a renewed period of persistent volatility. If food prices are no longer volatile, then policymakers may be losing useful information by omitting them.

## Recent Inflation Trends

In recent years, headline inflation has typically outpaced core inflation, as seen in *Figure 1*, because of the rapid rise in energy prices. In 2007, headline inflation was also driven up by a 3.9% increase in food prices. The difference between core and headline has not always been trivial — from 2003 to 2006, core inflation was 0.9 percentage points lower than headline. Considering that the Fed judges 2% inflation to be on the low side and 3% inflation on the high side, the definition used in these years would have arguably strongly colored their policy stance. The difference between core and headline inflation over this period was overwhelmingly the result of energy prices, which rose by an average of 12.8% a year as measured by the CPI.

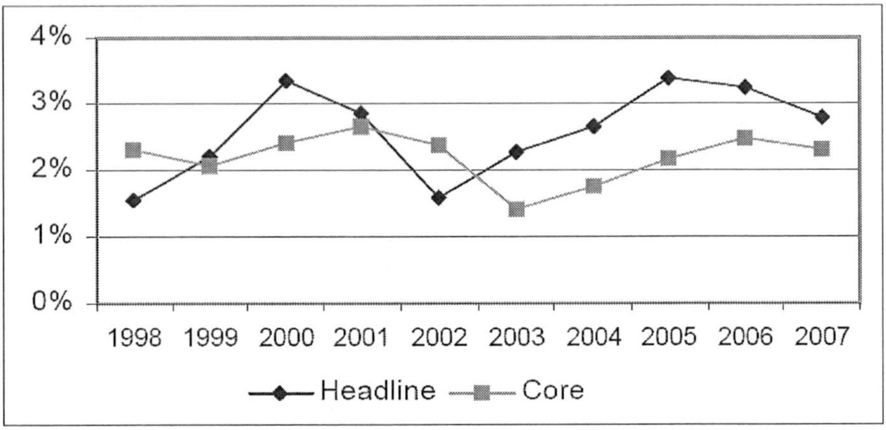


Source: Bureau of Labor Statistics.

Figure 1. Inflation Rate, 1998-2007.

## When Should Headline Inflation Be Used?

When comparing purchasing power over two time periods, headline inflation is the relevant measure. Comparisons over time of wages, wealth, rates of return, government transfers such as Social Security payments, and so on should all use a headline measure of inflation, because all of these concepts depend on a broad measure of inflation. For example, adjusting household income by core inflation would not be useful since food and energy consumption account for about one-quarter of average household expenditures. Similarly, government programs and parts of the tax code that are adjusted for inflation are based on headline inflation. Economic growth is also calculated by first adjusting GDP by headline inflation.

## When Should Core Inflation Be Used?

Core inflation is used by policymakers for the reason offered by Chairman Bernanke in the introduction — policymakers are most concerned about the future path of inflation, and current core inflation data may give better information than current headline data about future headline inflation. Headline inflation often does not have good predictive power over short-time periods because food and energy prices are so volatile. For example, the monthly headline inflation rate varied between -6.3% and 7.5% in 2006 at annualized rates, whereas the core rate varied between 1.2% and 3.6%.[8] Policymakers are concerned with future inflation because of lags between a change in policy and its effect on the economy. In essence, it is already too late for policy to influence current inflation, a policy change today can only affect future inflation.

Theoretically, short-term changes in inflation can be caused by the supply-side or demand-side of the economy. When rising inflation is demand-driven, it means that spending is growing too quickly in the overall economy, and production cannot keep pace. This phenomenon is captured in the famous saying "too much money chasing too few goods." The Fed's task is to counteract this by raising interest rates in order to reduce the growth rate of interest-sensitive spending. Likewise, if spending is rising too slowly, inflation will fall, which the Fed can counteract by reducing interest rates.

In the short run, the overall inflation rate can also be affected by sharp price changes of individual goods caused by supply shocks. For example, bad weather can drive up food prices or a reduction in the oil supply can drive up energy prices. Since these supply shocks are temporary, they should not have any lasting effect on inflation (holding aggregate spending constant), in which case they can be ignored by policymakers. In the long run, price shocks on the supply side should cancel each other out (since, across all goods, there will be an equal number of positive and negative surprises), and average inflation should be completely demand driven.

Ideally, policymakers would like to be able to identify whether any change in inflation was demand-driven or supply-driven. Unfortunately, there is no straightforward way to do this, so they have commonly used core inflation as a proxy for demand-driven inflation, reasoning that food and energy are two sectors of the economy that are most susceptible to supply shocks. Furthermore, policymakers are particularly concerned with inflationary expectations, and a rising core rate may be a better sign than rising headline that inflationary expectations have risen.

Relying on core inflation for policymaking has its drawbacks, however. There is no inherent reason that changes in food and energy prices cannot be caused by changes in aggregate demand. For example, rapid spending growth could push up energy prices if supply does not rise in response. In fact, an argument has been made that a change in aggregate demand would first show up in price changes of goods that have flexible pricing, such as commodities that are traded on financial markets where prices change continually to clear the market.[9] Both energy and basic foodstuffs are traded on financial markets, although the CPI measures final food and energy products, not basic commodities.

Furthermore, a rise in the price of any one good need not lead to a change in inflation if the prices of other goods fall to offset it. Technically, if a rise in one price leads to a rise in overall inflation, it must be because of some accommodation on the Fed's part (because it did not raise interest rates enough to induce other prices to fall). Most economists believe that some accommodation to relative price changes is desirable because it reduces the volatility of economic growth, whereas zero accommodation could lead to needless disruptions in economic activity. For example, Fed Governor Frederic Mishkin used the Fed's macro model of the U.S. economy to show that when the Fed reacts to changes in headline inflation instead of core inflation, future inflation will be slightly less volatile, but unemployment will be significantly more volatile.[10] But if the Fed accommodates a rise in the price of one good too much, then the price of all goods could start rising. In other words, a rise in headline inflation could feed through to higher core inflation. This scenario occurred in the 1970s where rising energy prices resulted in a rise in total inflation.

In scenarios like this one, a focus on core inflation could forestall a needed policy change until it is too late. Indeed, a case can be made today that more of a focus on headline inflation would have avoided the persistent upward trend in core inflation that has occurred from 2003 to 2007 and brought core inflation above the Fed's self-defined "comfort zone." The weakness with the focus on core inflation is that when energy prices rise continually for a period of several years, they no longer represent random price fluctuations that offer no useful information about future inflation. As a result, too much monetary policy accommodation may have taken place recently, causing the economy to overheat. Future events will reveal if this is the case, or if the rise in core inflation can be painlessly reversed without a recession.

In the end, the question of what measure of inflation is best for policymaking is an empirical one. One study found that "no core measure does an outstanding job forecasting [headline] CPI inflation...we find no strong evidence to suggest that a selected core measure will be able to retain its usefulness as a tool to forecast inflation for any given period..."[11] Another study did not find a statistically significant relationship between core inflation and future headline inflation, although the relationship becomes significant when limited to a more recent time period.[12] Two other studies found that headline inflation is a better predictor of future headline inflation than core inflation.[13] An explanation for this finding is that during the past 10 years, changes in core inflation have tended to lag behind changes in headline inflation as illustrated in *Figure 1*. One study found that a core measure that excludes only energy was a better predictor of future inflation from 1983 to 2001 than a measure excluding food and energy. In fact, that study found food prices to be a better predictor of future inflation than any other measure, including core inflation.[14] Some studies suggest that there may be more sophisticated measurements that are better gauges of underlying inflationary pressures than the standard definition of core inflation.[15] Core inflation has the advantage from a policy perspective, however, of being transparent, whereas the more sophisticated measurements could be hard for the public to understand and open to accusations of data mining or manipulation. While this advantage may make core inflation a useful tool for communicating Fed policy to the public, the empirical evidence suggests it to be, by itself, an inadequate tool for policymaking.

## End Note

[1] For more information, see CRS Report RL30344, *Inflation: Causes, Costs, and Current Status*, by Marc Labonte and Gail Makinen.

[2] For more information, see CRS Report RL30354, *Monetary Policy and the Federal Reserve*, by Marc Labonte and Gail Makinen.

[3] Chairman Ben S. Bernanke, "Panel Discussion: Comments on the Outlook for the U.S. Economy and Monetary Policy," at the International Monetary Conference, Washington, DC, June 5, 2006.

[4] For more information, see CRS Report RL30074, *The Consumer Price Index: A Brief Overview,* by Brian W. Cashell.

[5] Todd Clark, "Comparing Measures of Core Inflation," Federal Reserve Bank of Kansas City, *Economic Review*, 2002:2, p. 5. The four most volatile items are fuel oil, motor fuel, meats and dairy products, and fruits and vegetables.

[6] Seamus Smyth, "Why Care About Core?," Goldman Sachs, *U.S. Daily Financial Market Comment*, September 7, 2006.

[7] William Gavin and Rachel Mandal, "Predicting Inflation: Food for Thought," Federal Reserve Bank of St. Louis, *Regional Economist*, January 2002.

[8] Of course, volatility is lower over longer time horizons, so policymakers also judge inflationary pressures by looking at, say, the 12-month change in inflation rather than the one-month change. In 2006, the 12-month change in headline inflation varied between 1.3% to 4.3%, and 12-month core inflation varied between 2.1% and 2.9%.

[9] Brian Motley, "Should Monetary Policy Focus on Core Inflation?," Federal Reserve Bank of San Francisco, *Economic Letter*, no. 97-11, April 1997.

[10] Frederic Mishkin, "Headline versus Core Inflation in the Conduct of Monetary Policy," speech at the Business Cycles, International Transmission and Macroeconomic Policies Conference, Montreal, Canada, October 20, 2007.

[11] Robert Rich and Charles Steindel, "A Review of Core Inflation and an Evaluation of Its Measures," Federal Reserve Bank of New York, staff report no. 236, December 2005. The study examines the forecasting power of inflation less food and energy, as well as alternative definitions of core inflation that have been proposed by others.

[12] Todd Clark, "Comparing Measures of Core Inflation," Federal Reserve Bank of Kansas City, *Economic Review*, 2002:2, p. 5.

[13] Michael Bryan and Stephen Cecchetti, "Measuring Core Inflation," in N. Gregory Mankiw, ed., *Monetary Policy* (Chicago: University of Chicago Press, 1994), p. 195; and Julie Smith, "Weighted Median Inflation: Is This Core Inflation?," *Journal of Money, Credit, and Banking*, April 2004, vol. 36, no. 2, p. 253. Both studies compared the forecasting ability of many measures of inflation, and concluded that a weighted median measure of inflation performed best.

[14] William Gavin and Rachel Mandal, "Predicting Inflation: Food for Thought," Federal Reserve Bank of St. Louis, *Regional Economist*, January 2002.

[15] Economists have tried to find the best measure of core inflation according to different criteria. See Timothy Cogley, "A Simple Adaptive Measure of Core Inflation," *Journal of Money, Credit and Banking,* vol. 34, no. 1, February 2002, pp. 94-113; Danny Quah; Shaun P. Vahey, "Measuring Core Inflation," *The Economic Journal,* vol. 105, no. 432, September 1995, pp. 1130-1144; Michael Bryan and Stephen Cecchetti, "Measuring Core Inflation," in N. Gregory Mankiw, ed., *Monetary Policy*, (Chicago: University of Chicago Press, 1994), p. 195; Todd Clark, "Comparing Measures of Core Inflation," Federal Reserve Bank of Kansas City, *Economic Review*, 2002:2, p. 5.

In: Inflation and the Consumer Price Index ISBN: 978-1-61942-705-1
Editors: E. L. Green, A. N. Walker 

*Chapter 4*

# CONSUMERS AND FOOD PRICE INFLATION*

***Randy Schnepf and Joe Richardson***

## SUMMARY

The heightened commodity price volatility of 2008 and 2010 and the subsequent acceleration in U.S. food price inflation associated with those market shifts raised concerns and generated many questions about farm and food price movements by Members of Congress and their constituents. This report responds to those concerns by addressing the nature and measurement of retail food price inflation.

During the 1991 to 2006 period, U.S. food prices were fairly stable—annual food price inflation, as measured by the U.S. Bureau of Labor Statistics (BLS) Consumer Price Index (CPI) for all food (excluding alcoholic beverages), averaged a relatively low 2.5%. However, several economic factors emerged in late 2005 that began to gradually push market prices higher for both raw agricultural commodities and energy costs, and ultimately retail food prices. U.S. food price inflation increased at a rate of 4% in 2007 and at 5.5% in 2008—the highest since 1990 and well above the general inflation rate of 3.8%.

By late 2008 the inflationary price trends had reversed. Prices for many raw agricultural commodities had already started to decline by late spring of 2008; however, owing to lags in the adjustment process, it was not until November 2008 that monthly food price inflation fell to near 0%, and it actually declined from February through May 2009.

* This is an edited, reformatted and augmented version of a Congressional Research Service publication, CRS Report for Congress R40545, from www.crs.gov, dated April 14, 2011.

Annual food price inflation dropped from 5.5% in 2008 to 1.8% in 2009. Although the price inflation trend reversed itself in mid-2009, average annual food price inflation continued to fall hitting 0.8% in 2010. USDA projects that annual food price inflation will accelerate into a range of 3%-4% in 2011 as surging commodity and energy costs drive inflation higher in the latter half of 2011.

The all-food CPI has two components—food-at-home and food-away-from-home. The food-athome CPI is most representative of retail food prices and is significantly more volatile than the food-away-from-home index. The food-at-home CPI is projected in a range of 3.5% to 4.5% for 2011, compared with a 3% to 4% annual inflation rate for food-away-from home prices. This difference is partially explained by the larger share of farm products in the final price of retail foods than in food-away-from home. Farm product prices are, in general, substantially more volatile than the other marketing and processing costs that enter into retail or ready-to-eat foods.

Many wages and salaries, as well as federal programs (including several domestic food assistance programs), are linked to price inflation through escalation clauses in order to retain their purchasing power. For households where income and federal benefits do not keep up with price inflation, declines in purchasing power are real and immediate. However, even for households with escalation clauses, a time lag usually occurs between the time the price inflation is measured and the time when the wage or program benefit is adjusted upward to compensate.

The 2008-2009 global economic crisis—which encompassed higher retail prices, unemployment, income loss, and lower effective household purchasing power—resulted in higher participation rates in the federal food and nutrition programs. The past decade has seen a tremendous expansion in use of USDA's food and nutrition assistance programs—federal expenditures totaled $94.8 billion in FY2010 and marked the 10$^{th}$ consecutive year in which food and nutrition assistance expenditures exceeded the previous historical record. Since FY2004, expenditures for food and nutrition assistance have more than doubled.

## INTRODUCTION

Everyone eats. As a result, everyone is affected to some degree by food price changes. This makes understanding food price changes and their effects on consumers an important matter for Congress. This report provides information on the current status and outlook for U.S. food prices, measuring their changes and how such changes relate to U.S. consumers.

The first section of the report, "Consumer Demand," briefly reviews the major economic concepts underlying consumer food behavior. The second section, the "Consumer Price Index," describes how U.S. food price inflation rates have evolved since 1915, when federal price data collection for inflation-measuring purposes began. The third section, "Consumer Income and Expenditures," provides information on recent history and projections for U.S. food expenditure shares relative to total household budget, with comparisons across income quintiles, as well as internationally. The fourth section, "Recent Food Price Inflation," examines retail food price inflation, including a review and discussion of the level of food price inflation registered by the consumer price index for all-food, at-home, and away-from-home food purchases as well as for major food groups. Finally, a fifth section, entitled "Effect of High Prices," discusses the impact that rapid food price inflation can have on government food programs and the more vulnerable consumer groups.

Each section may be read independently of the others. Thus, those readers that are concerned primarily with the status of U.S. food price inflation may proceed directly to the sections entitled "Historic Price Inflation Patterns" or "Recent Food Price Inflation."

## Consumer Demand

Consumer demand is influenced by economic factors—own-price, the price of close substitutes, the price of complementary items, and household income—as well as by several non-economic factors including tastes and preferences, family size, age of family members, geographic location, shopping behavior, and lifestyle choices. Economists attempt to study and measure the nature of consumer behavior in response to changes in prices, incomes, and household characteristics, with an eye for understanding the potential social welfare outcomes that may result from price and income changes across different socioeconomic groups. Policymakers, in turn, often attempt to use that information to design and implement policies that mitigate the more deleterious effects of price and income changes on consumers.

### Price Responsiveness

In general, consumers will use less of any good if its price increases relative to other goods (referred to as the pure "substitution effect" by economists). However, a consumer's price responsiveness is a matter of degree and is subject to the potential influence of disposable income as well as other non-price factors such as those listed in the preceding paragraph.

Under most circumstances, the availability of many close substitutes is likely to make consumers more sensitive or responsive to price changes, because they have the opportunity to switch to similar alternatives. In contrast, a lack of substitutes may give the consumer little choice but to continue to purchase the available good, even as its price rises, especially if it is deemed a necessity. Strong ethnic or cultural tastes and preferences may endear a person to a particular food type such that he or she will continue to purchase that food as its price rises even in the presence of abundant substitutes (for example, ethnic groups that are accustomed to eating rice at every meal may be reluctant to switch to bread or potatoes even if the price of rice rises relative to those other foods).

Rapid or unexpected changes in retail food prices will impact some consumers more than others depending on income levels and the importance of the affected food items in consumers' budgets. In general, if an item represents a very small portion of the consumer's budget (for example, consider salt), then a consumer is less likely to respond to a price change. Basic food staples such as bread, potatoes, pasta, and rice tend to take smaller shares of the consumer's food budget (relative to meat, dairy products, fruits and vegetables, and more processed food products) and, as a result, consumers are less responsive to a change in their price. In contrast, high-valued food items such as expensive cuts of meat or seafood probably represent more costly (and infrequently purchased) delicacies for most households. As a result, most households will tend to be far more responsive to changes in the prices of such high-valued products than for basic staples. Often a price change for an item within a specific food group[1] may result in consumers switching to lower-quality items within that food category—the classic example being a switch from steak to hamburger when meat prices rise. In contrast, a widespread price rise across all food groups may engender substantial reshuffling of consumer food budget allocations as households try to meet their nutritional goals with their limited budgets.

Of course, the absolute size of a consumer's disposable income is also important in determining actual purchasing power. For households with smaller incomes, the food budget itself is likely a larger portion of total household expenditures, and such households are likely to be more responsive to price changes across all food categories than are higher-income households.

In summary, lower-income consumers who spend a significant share of their household budget on food are likely to be impacted more severely by rising food prices (and are likely to be more responsive to price changes) than high-income consumers with lower food budget shares.

## Income Responsiveness

A household's absolute level of disposable income (and, to a lesser degree, wealth) directly affects its ability to respond to price changes. As a result, as household incomes grow, consumers often opt for more expensive or higher-quality selections of foods than are presently in their food budget, or may experiment by trying new or unfamiliar foods. For example, as incomes increase in less-developed countries, it is common to see per-capita expenditures on meat and dairy products increase. In contrast, when incomes decline, consumers tend to pull back from more expensive options. If the income decline is severe and is perceived as permanent or long-lasting, consumers may make substantial changes to their food budget choices.

In the aggregate, household consumption behavior in response to perceived income changes (if persistent and widespread) may affect a country's agricultural production or trade patterns, or it may impact the health and nutritional status of certain segments of the population. As a result, it is important for policymakers to monitor household wealth and income levels and distribution for unexpected shifts that may have important economic or health consequences.

Economists call the relationship between changes in consumer income and the quantity of an item purchased an *Engel curve*. This relationship is used by economists to classify goods.

- For a *normal good*, consumers buy more of it as their incomes increase, but at a decreasing rate such that its average budget share declines for higher income levels.
- For a *luxury good*, consumers buy more of it as their incomes increase and at an increasing rate such that its budget share increases at higher income levels.
- For an *inferior good,* consumers buy less of it as their incomes increase.

Of course, different goods will be classified differently by different people since tastes and preferences also are important. However, with respect to the overall food budget, in the aggregate certain behavioral norms are expected. *Engel's law* is the idea (largely validated by data with some minor exceptions) that food, in general, is a normal good, so that the budget share spent on food declines as a consumer's income rises. While Engel's law is generally observable for individual households, it tends to hold best in the aggregate—that is, when considering an entire population. To the extent that this "law" holds, then the proportion of a nation's income spent on food serves as a good index for international comparisons of relative consumer welfare (*Table 3*).

## Tastes and Preferences

Non-economic factors such as cultural or ethnic preferences may determine both the share of a particular food product in the household's budget (e.g., rice represents a larger share of per-capita expenditure in most Asian households than in most European households at similar income levels) as well as a household's responsiveness to a change in the price of a particular product.

Dietary needs also change with age. For example, young children and adolescents generally need both more calories and a higher portion of protein-based calories to meet nutritional demands of rapid physical growth and high activity levels. Populations or households with a large share of individuals from this demographic stratum are more likely to consume larger per-capita portions of meat and dairy products than an older, more mature and sedentary population would. As a result, population demographics such as household composition, size, and age structure often play an important role in consumer price sensitivity and income responsiveness. In increasingly affluent societies, lifestyle choices, when complemented with sufficient purchasing power, can also play an influential role in household food purchases.

## Summary

For households with low disposable income levels where food expenditures are a large share of the budget, rising food prices result in greater responsiveness and may force more difficult budgetary tradeoffs than in higher-income households with smaller food-budget shares. Of course the opposite effect is true during periods of falling prices. However, each household's price and income effects also are influenced by its particular set of non-economic characteristics.

## The Consumer Price Index (CPI)

The CPI is perhaps the most widely reported measure of U.S. price inflation.[2] The CPI is used both as an economic indicator of retail price inflation and as a means of adjusting current-period values for inflation. The "All-Items" CPI is the index most often referred to (i.e., the headline CPI) for representing consumer price inflation. It is generally divided into eight major spending categories, including a "Food and Beverage" category.

The CPI category of "Food and Beverages" is composed of two major subcategories: "All-Food" (which has a relative weight of 14.6% in the all-items CPI), and "Alcoholic Beverages" (1.1%). The all-food CPI is the principal indicator of consumer food price changes. The all-food CPI can be subdivided into the "Food-at-Home" and "Food-Away-from-Home" categories. The *food-athome CPI* reflects changes in the prices of foods consumed at home. As such it is the principal indicator of changes in retail food prices in the United States. The *food-away-from-home CPI* reflects changes in the prices of foods purchased outside of the home, primarily at eating and drinking places such as restaurants and other eating establishments. However, it also includes price changes for ready-to-eat foods purchased at hotels and motels, recreational places and sporting events, vending machines, and school and work cafeterias.

### Historic Price Inflation Patterns

Over time, the all-food and all-items CPIs have moved together, although the all-food CPI has been consistently more variable than the all-items CPI (*Figure 1* and *Table 1*). Prior to 1960, both of these indexes exhibited higher average inflation rates and more volatility than in recent years. During the 1914-1920 period, both price indexes recorded double-digit annual inflation. Food inflation hit its all-time high of 28.7% in 1917 (*Figure 1*). All-items price inflation peaked a year later at 18%. Just four years later retail prices entered a prolonged deflationary period, starting in 1921 with a deflationary plunge of -24.2% for all-food and -10.5% for all-items, that lasted until 1941 when war time shortages finally renewed retail price inflation.

The variability of the overall CPI and its individual components is important because uncertainty about price changes makes planning more difficult—whether it is the investment planning of a business, the meal planning of a household, or the policy intervention planning of a government agency.

During the 1941-1960 period, price inflation remained extremely volatile, alternating between spikes of inflation and steep disinflationary (i.e., deflationary) drops. It was not until 1960 that retail prices stabilized with tolerably mild inflation. However, this proved short-lived as the 1970s saw a return to sharp price spikes generated by an energy crisis and rapid, unexpected shifts in global crop supply and demand.[3] By the early 1980s, retail price inflation had returned to modest levels below 5%. Since 1983 retail prices, as measured by the all-items and the all-food CPIs, have been relatively low and relatively stable, except for temporary surges in 1989-1990 and again in 2007-2008.

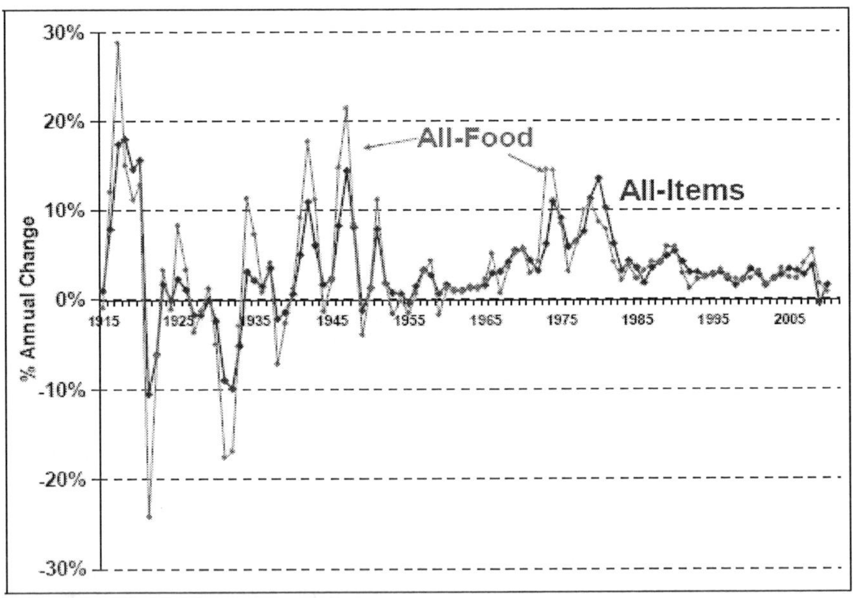


Source: Department of Labor, Bureau of Labor Statistics.

Notes: The percent change is calculated from the annual average CPI for successive years.

Figure 1. Annual Price Inflation, 1915-2010: All-Items vs. All-Food.

**Table 1. Retail Price Change, Mean and Variability, by Historic Time Period (all data—mean and standard deviation (SD)—are percentages)**

| | 1914-1920 | | 1921-1941 | | 1941-1960 | | 1960-1983 | | 1983-2010 | |
|---|---|---|---|---|---|---|---|---|---|---|
| | Mean | SD | Mean | SD | Mean | SD | Mean | SD | Mean | SD |
| All-Items | 10.8 | 7.4 | -1.4 | 4.5 | 3.9 | 4.1 | 5.3 | 3.6 | 3.0 | 1.2 |
| Energy | — | — | — - | — | — | — | 6.9 | 9.1 | 3.1 | 8.1 |
| All-Food | 11.6 | 9.6 | 1.8 | 9.0 | 4.9 | 7.2 | 5.2 | 4.1 | 3.0 | 1.3 |
| At-Home | — | — | — | — | — | — | 5.0 | 4.5 | 2.9 | 1.7 |
| Away-from-Home | —— | — — | —— | — — | —— | — — | 6.0 | 3.1 | 3.1 | 1.0 |
| Core[a] | | | | | | | 5.1 | 3.3 | 3.0 | 1.2 |

Source: Calculations were made by CRS based on BLS CPI data.

Notes: ”—“ = not available. The mean is the average annual price change for each period. The standard deviation (SD) is a measure of dispersion around the mean value for each period. Plus or minus one (two) SD captures 68.2% (95.4%) of the variation around the mean value for each period. The mean and SD have been calculated using the annual percent change data for each of the five different periods. A larger SD implies greater variability, for example, all-food price inflation has shown a clear pattern of declining variability as the SD has fallen from 9.6% during the 1914-20 period to 4.1% during 1960-83 (more than halving the variability), and finally to 1.3% during 1983-2010 (a further decline of over 70% in variability).

[a]. The “Core” price index is the all-items CPI without the energy and all-food components.

## Overall Inflation versus Core Inflation

Many economists and policymakers believe that the food and energy components of the CPI are volatile and subject to shocks not easily dealt with through government monetary policy. In response, the BLS also reports another price index, referred to as the “core” index because it removes the food and energy price components from the all-items CPI.[4] The so-called core CPI is thought to be a useful measure of underlying trend inflation in the short run. According to BLS data, the food component of the CPI, although more volatile than the overall CPI, is still substantially less volatile than the energy component (*Figure 2* and *Table 1*).

Since 1960, the energy price index has been a more volatile component of the all-items CPI than the food price index by a substantial margin. For example, the energy price inflation standard deviation (SD) of 9.1% was more than double the all-food SD of 4.1% during the 1960-1983 period, and nearly six times larger since 1983 (8.1% versus 1.3%).

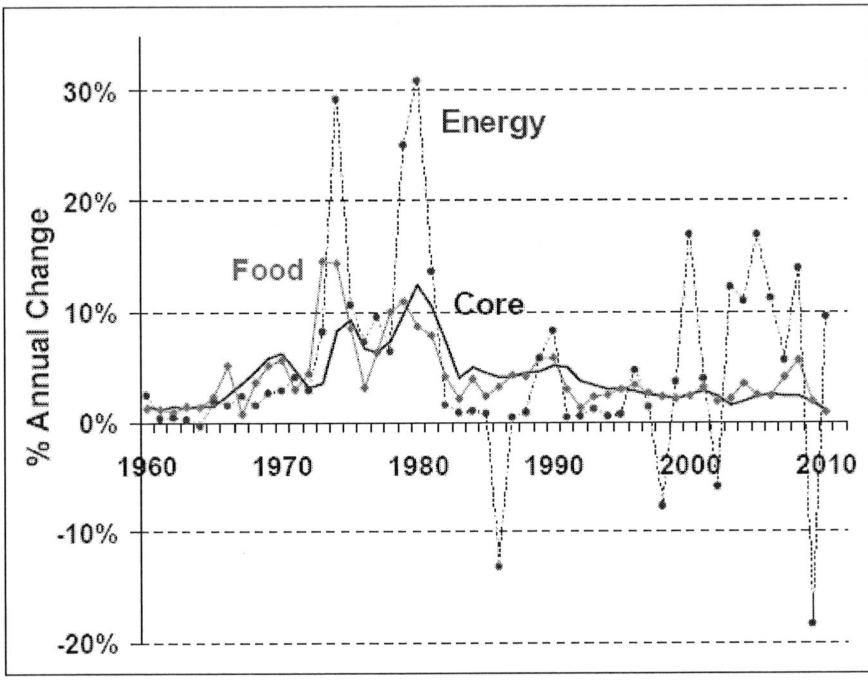


Source: Department of Labor, Bureau of Labor Statistics.

Figure 2. Annual Price Inflation Since 1960: All-Items, All-Food, and Energy.

Since 1983 both the all-food and the all-items CPIs have been lower (in terms of average values) and substantially more stable (in terms of SDs) than during the preceding seven decades. In contrast, the energy price index has remained nearly as volatile since 1983 (although at a lower mean level) as it was during the preceding two decades.

This is an important point because the energy price index has seen its weighted share of the CPI gradually increase over time and, although energy's current weight share of 7.6% is only about half that of the food weight share of 14.6%, energy price inflation is far more insidious than food inflation to the extent that energy costs figure in the retail price of practically every other component of the CPI.

# CONSUMER INCOME AND EXPENDITURES

A household allocates its available income across a range of expenditure, savings, and investment choices. As mentioned earlier, food expenditures as a share of a household's total budget are an indicator of sensitivity (or vulnerability) to unexpected food price changes. At the national level, food budget share (via Engel's law) can be used as a general indicator of welfare among nations.

## Food as a Share of Consumer's Budget

According to Bureau of Economic Analysis (BEA) estimates, in 2009 total U.S. disposable personal income (DPI) was $11,035 billion, or $35,985 per capita.[5] Of these estimates, ERS calculates that, on average, 9.4% of disposable personal income was spent on food.[6]

*Figure 3* shows the evolution of the average food budget share against U.S. DPI per capita in constant 1982-1984 average dollars. By both measures (food budget share and real DPI per capita), U.S. consumers have seen their "well-being" improve substantially over the past 70 years. (Note that these are national averages that ignore any potential distribution issues.) The U.S. food share of real DPI has fallen from a high of 25.2% in 1933 to under 10% since 2000, while the average DPI per capita (in 1982-1984 dollars) has risen from $3,629 in 1933 to over $16,000 by 2004.

When measured as a share of average total consumer expenditures of $49,067 per household (based on Consumer Expenditure Survey (CES) data, *Table 2*), average food outlays of $6,372 per household accounted for 13.0% of total spending in 2009.[7] As mentioned earlier, the difference between the two estimates of food budget share (9.4% based on DPI versus 13.0% based on CES total expenditures) is due to how disposable income and food expenditures are calculated for each of these indicators.

The estimated food share of household expenditures (*Table 2*) varied across income quintiles in the United States, in accordance with Engel's law—that is, each succeeding higher income quintile increased its absolute expenditures on food (in dollar terms), but at a decreasing rate such that the food budget share declines across higher quintiles. For example, the lowest 20% of U.S. households spent $3,501 on food, or 16.2% of their average total expenditures of $21,611 in 2009. The budget food outlay increases in absolute dollars, while the food budget share declines across income quintiles until the wealthiest quintile, where households spent an average of $10,780 on food, or 11.4% of their total budget of $94,244.

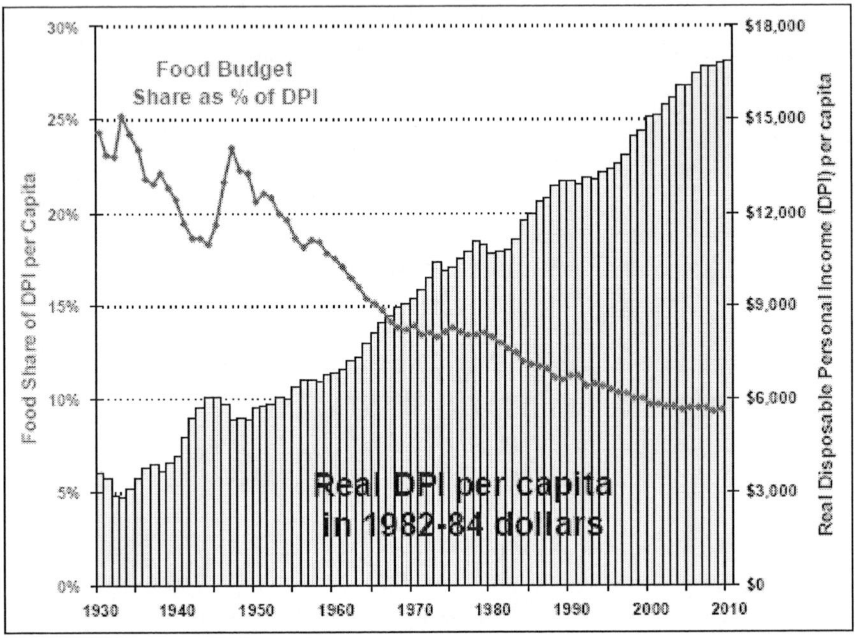


Source: "Food CPI, Prices and Expenditures Briefing Room," Food Expenditure Tables, ERS, USDA.

Notes: Real DPI is BEA nominal DPI series deflated by the all-items CPI with base 1982-1984 = 100; real food expenditures are the ERS series of food expenditures deflated by the all-food CPI with base 1982-1984 = 100.

Figure 3. Comparison of Real U.S. Disposable Personal Income (DPI) Per Capita and the Share of DPI Spent on Food, 1930-2010.

Another clear pattern that emerges from the CES data (*Table 2*) is the propensity to spend more of the food budget on away-from-home food consumption at higher income levels, both in absolute dollars and as a share of the food budget (refer to the percentages in parentheses in *Table 2*), thereby meeting the description of a luxury good. Or, otherwise stated, lower-income U.S. households tend to spend a larger share of their food budget on at-home consumption and are thus more vulnerable to unexpected retail food price increases (this is discussed further in the next section).

**Table 2. Average Household Food Expenditures in 2009 by Income Quintiles**

| Income Quintile | Total | All Food | | | Food-at-Home | Food-Away-from-Home | |
|---|---|---|---|---|---|---|---|
| | | | Expenditures per Household | | | | |
| Highest 20% | $94,244 | $10,780 | 11.4% | $5,629 | 6.0% | $5,151 | 5.5% |
| Fourth 20% | $56,879 | $7,522 | 13.2% | $4,316 | 7.6% | $3,206 | 5.6% |
| Third 20% | $41,150 | $5,483 | 13.3% | $3,355 | 8.2% | $2,127 | 5.2% |
| Second 20% | $31,382 | $4,569 | 14.6% | $2,999 | 9.6% | $1,569 | 5.0% |
| Lowest 20% | $21,611 | $3,501 | 16.2% | $2,463 | 11.4% | $1,038 | 4.8% |
| Average Outlay ($) | $49,067 | $6,372 | 13.0% | $3,753 | 7.6% | $2,619 | 5.3% |
| Highest 20% | | 100% | | 52.2% | | 47.8% | |
| Fourth 20% | | 100% | | 57.4% | | 42.6% | |
| Third 20% | | 100% | | 61.2% | | 38.8% | |
| Second 20% | | 100% | | 65.6% | | 34.3% | |
| Lowest 20% | | 100% | | 70.4% | | 29.6% | |
| Average Outlay (%) | | 100% | | 58.9% | | 41.1% | |

Source: Table 1. Quintiles of before-tax income: Average annual expenditures and characteristics, Consumer Expenditure Survey, 2009, BLS, Dept. of Labor, at http://www.bls.gov/cex/2009/Standard/quintile.pdf.

## At-Home versus Away-from-Home Consumption

U.S. households have shown a strong propensity over time to increase their share of annual food consumption outside of the home (*Figure 4*). This tendency is associated with increasing per-capita disposable income as mentioned above. It is also associated with increasing female participation in the labor force, more two-earner households, increased advertising and promotion by large food-service chains, increasing time constraints on household members (e.g., longer commutes, increased work hours and less leisure time, etc.), the smaller size of U.S. households, and the increased availability of relatively low-cost fast food establishments.[8]

With the exception of a brief period following the end of World War II, the portion of the national food budget spent on food consumption away from the home has steadily increased from 9% in 1900 to an estimated 49% in 2010. This phenomenon has important implications for consumer responsiveness to price and income changes, as well as for household nutrition.

The prices of food-at-home purchases are significantly more volatile than are prices of food-away-from-home purchases (*Table 1* and *Figure 5*). ERS research suggests that away-from-home expenditures are typically higher for single-person households and households containing multiple adults without living-at-home children.[9] By implication, households with living-at-home children typically rely more on at-home food consumption (as a share of their budget) and are thus more vulnerable to the normally higher price variability associated with retail food prices.

Although increased food-away-from-home expenditure is associated with higher income (both in absolute terms and as a share of the household food budget), it is not always a luxury item. A partial key to understanding how increasing food-away-from-home consumption may impact consumer behavior is the extent to which such consumption is a choice (for example, made in the evenings or on weekends during leisure hours) or more of an obligation (made during work hours), as well as the extent to which a consumer has alternative dining choices when eating out (for example, subsidized cafeteria meals are often available at schools or in large institutional work settings).

## International Comparisons

The Economic Research Service (ERS) includes in its food expenditure data series a comparison of food budget shares (based on at-home food expenditures) for over 70 countries. *Table 3* includes samples of countries from the ERS database ranked in terms of their at-home food expenditure budget shares, from smallest to largest. These data suggest that, on average, the United States has achieved a higher level of social welfare (based on this particular indicator) than any of the other countries in the database.

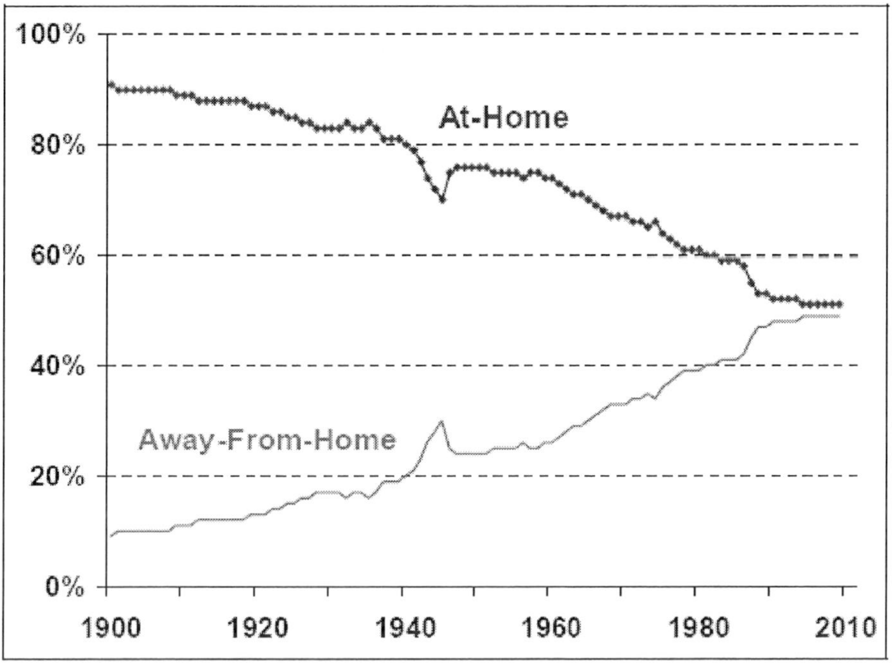


Source: Table 7, "Food CPI, Prices and Expenditures Briefing Room," Food Expenditure Tables, ERS, USDA, available at http://www.ers.usda.gov/Briefing/CPIFoodAndExpenditures/Data/.

Figure 4. Average U.S. Food Expenditure Shares: At-Home vs. Away-from-Home.

The food budget share is only one indicator of national welfare, and it ignores any unfavorable distribution of the food expenditure share (should any exist). Referring back to *Table 2* for the at-home food budget share for U.S. income and total expenditure quintiles based on CES data, it would appear that even the lowest 20% of U.S. households, on average, spend less than 12% of their budgets on at-home food consumption and thus appear relatively well-off in food terms based on this particular international standard. Readers should note that this cursory assessment is aggregate in nature and does not exclude the possibility that there are food-deficient individuals within the lowest 20% quintile of the U.S. population. According to ERS, in 2009, an estimated 14.7% of U.S. households were food-insecure at least some time during the course of the year.[10]

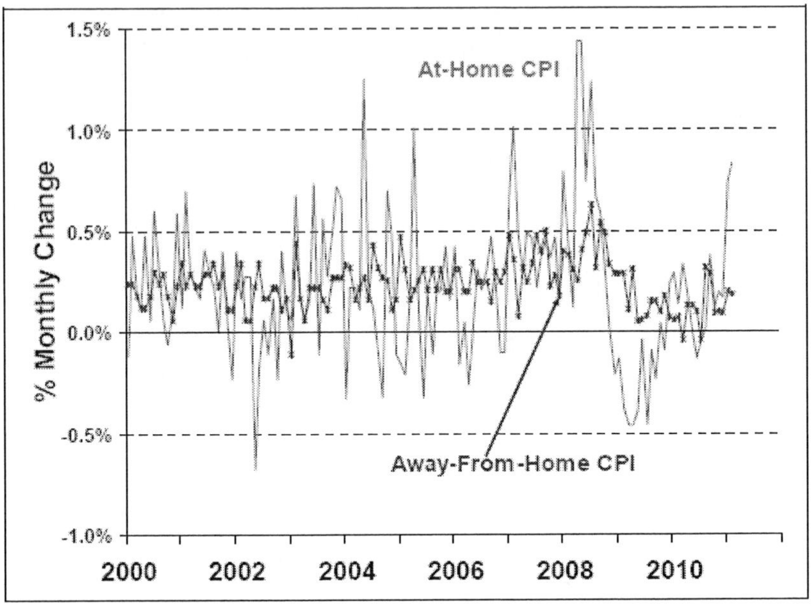


Source: BLS, U.S. Dept. of Labor.

Notes: Month-to-month inflation measured as the percent change in the monthly seasonally adjusted CPI for each index.

Figure 5. Monthly Food Price Inflation Since 2000: At-Home vs. Away-from-Home.

# Recent Food Price Inflation

This section provides a discussion of observed food price inflation in recent years based on CPI data. It is important to remember that the various CPI categories discussed here are indicative of price changes at the retail level in U.S. urban settings. As such, they are indicative of the prices faced by most consumers living in the United States (approximately 87% of U.S. consumers are covered by the CPI data collection process).

## Annual All-Food versus All-Items Price Inflation

As a general rule, the all-item and all-food CPIs tend to move together. Following a relatively tumultuous period of price inflation in the late 1980s, both price indexes entered an extended period of relative stability. From 1991 through 2006, the all-food CPI measured average annual inflation of 2.5%, compared with 2.7% annual average all-items price inflation.

**Table 3. International Comparison of Food-at-Home Budget Shares, Selected Countries, 2009**

| Country | Total Expenditures per capita | At-Home Food Expenditures per capita | At-Home Food Share |
|---|---|---|---|
| United States | $32,051 | $1,979 | 6.2% |
| United Kingdom | $21,788 | $1,928 | 8.8% |
| Canada | $23,088 | $2,091 | 9.1% |
| Germany | $22,812 | $2,596 | 11.4% |
| France | $24,271 | $3,268 | 13.5% |
| Japan | $22,909 | $3,260 | 14.2% |
| Italy | $21,253 | $3,026 | 14.2% |
| South Korea | $8,865 | $1,341 | 15.1% |
| Poland | $6,910 | $1,405 | 20.3% |
| Mexico | $5,501 | $1,319 | 24.0% |
| Brazil | $45118 | $1,265 | 24.7% |
| Russia | $4,572 | $1,280 | 28.0% |
| China | $1,257 | $414 | 32.9% |
| India | $620 | $219 | 35.4% |
| Philippines | $1,278 | $469 | 36.7% |
| Egypt | $2,111 | $805 | 38.1% |
| Nigeria | $631 | $252 | 39.9% |
| Indonesia | $1,357 | $583 | 43.0% |
| Algeria | $1,305 | $571 | 43.8% |
| Pakistan | $681 | $309 | 45.5% |

Source: Table 97, "Food CPI, Prices and Expenditures Briefing Room," Food Expenditure Tables, ERS, USDA, available at http://www.ers.usda.gov/Briefing/CPIFoodAndExpenditures/Data/.

However, several economic factors emerged in late 2005 that began to gradually push market prices higher for both raw agricultural commodities and energy costs.[11] These factors included rising consumer incomes, not just in the United States but globally, which sparked demand for meat and dairy products, food and feed grains, and raw materials ranging from minerals and metals to coal and petroleum. In 2007, U.S. food price inflation reached 4% (*Figure 7*), the highest since 1990.

In early 2008, monthly food price inflation began to accelerate (*Figure 8*). In July 2008, the month-to-month food price change was 0.96% (equivalent to an annual rate of 12.1% if sustained for the entire year). Monthly retail food price inflation responds with a lag of several months to price changes in raw commodity markets. For the entire year, 2008 food prices rose by 5.5%, well above the all-items CPI of 3.8% (*Figure 6*).

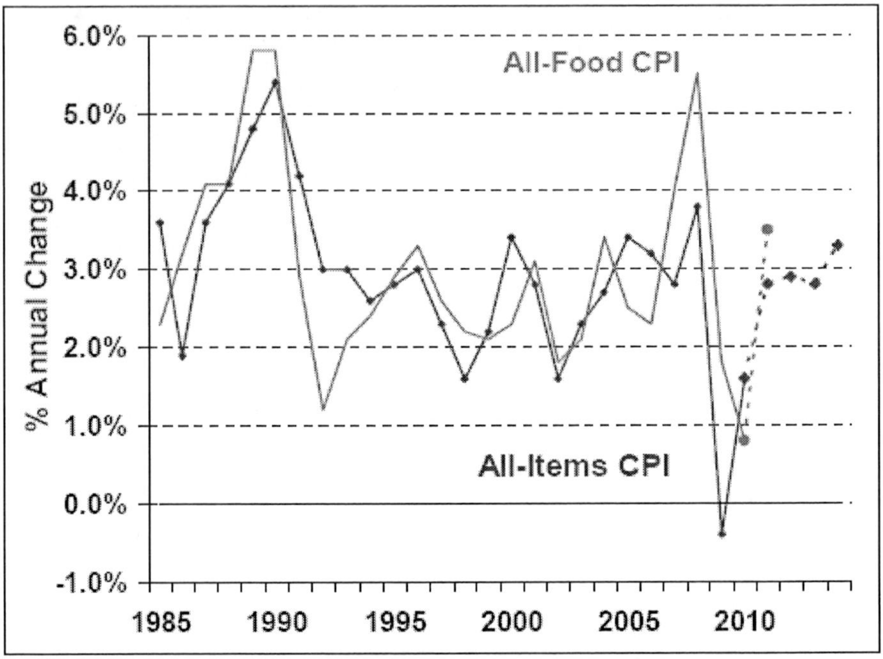


Source: Historical data, adjusted for seasonality, For 1985-2010, data are from the Dept. of Labor, BLS. Data for 2011 all-food CPI are from USDA, ERS, as of March 25, 2011; all-items CPI data for 2011to 2014 are from Global Insights, U.S. Economic Outlook, April 2011.

Notes: The percent change is calculated from the annual average CPI for successive years.

Figure 6. Annual Price Inflation: All-Items vs. All-Food, 1985-2014F.

### *The 2011 Forecast for Annual Food Price Inflation*

In late 2008 the financial crisis hit U.S. markets leading to a severe economic recession. Retail price trends reversed themselves and began following prices for raw agricultural commodities, which had already started to decline by late spring of 2008. Annual food price inflation dropped from 5.5% in 2008 to 1.8% in 2009. Although the price inflation trend reversed itself in mid-2009, average annual food price inflation continued to fall, hitting 0.8% in 2010 (*Figure 7*).[12]

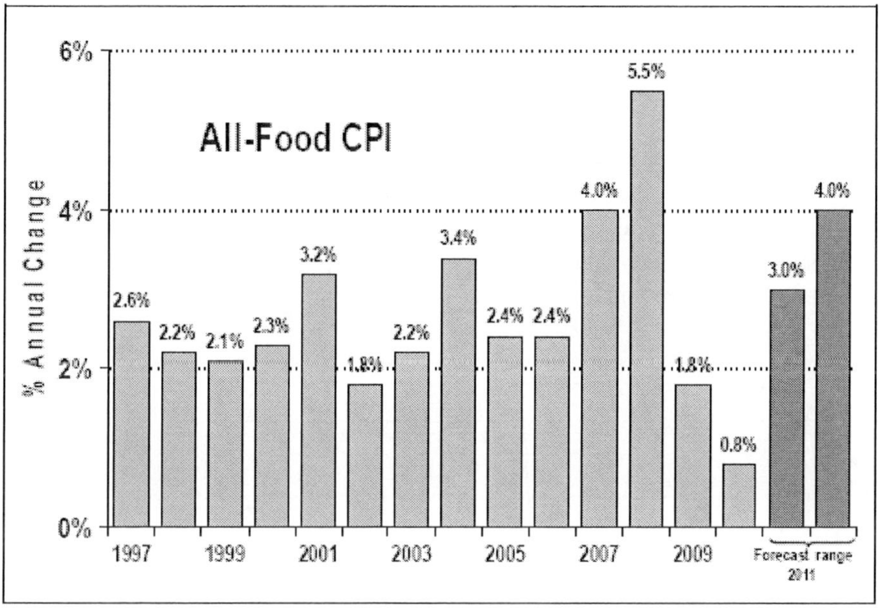


Source: Historical data (1985-2010) are from the Dept. of Labor, BLS. Forecast for the 2011 all-food CPI is from USDA, ERS, March 25, 2011.

Figure 7. Annual Food Price Inflation Since 1997.

Sharply lower commodity and energy costs combined with weak domestic and global economies to reduce inflationary pressures from 2008 levels for both the all-items and all-food price indexes. However, the all-items CPI was subject to much stronger deflationary pressures than the all-food CPI. As a result, the disparity between the two indexes widened in 2009 as the all-items CPI fell at an annual rate of -0.4% (*Figure 6*). By late 2009 global economies resumed growing followed in 2010 by a gradual return growth in the U.S. economy, thus reversing the deflationary price pattern. Recovering U.S. and global economies, coupled with tight commodity market supply and demand conditions, are expected to push food price inflation upward into the 3% to 4% range in 2011.

### *The Recent Monthly All-Food Price Inflation Pattern*

When the all-food CPI is adjusted for seasonal variations and expressed on a monthly basis, four strong patterns can be seen to have emerged since January 2007 (Figure 8). First, a mildly volatile, downward pattern of monthly price change persisted throughout 2007. This was followed by a highly volatile, upward pattern of price inflation during the first half of 2008. At this point the financial crisis struck and monthly price changes declined sharply. By November 2008 monthly retail food price inflation had fallen to near 0% (see Figure 8), then in December they actually fell below the preceding month's level (i.e., the monthly all-food CPI deflated or become negative) for the first time since November 2006. Monthly food price changes continued their deflationary trend hitting bottom in May of 2009. Finally, food prices have shown an upward trend since May 2009 as both global and U.S. economic activity regains strength.

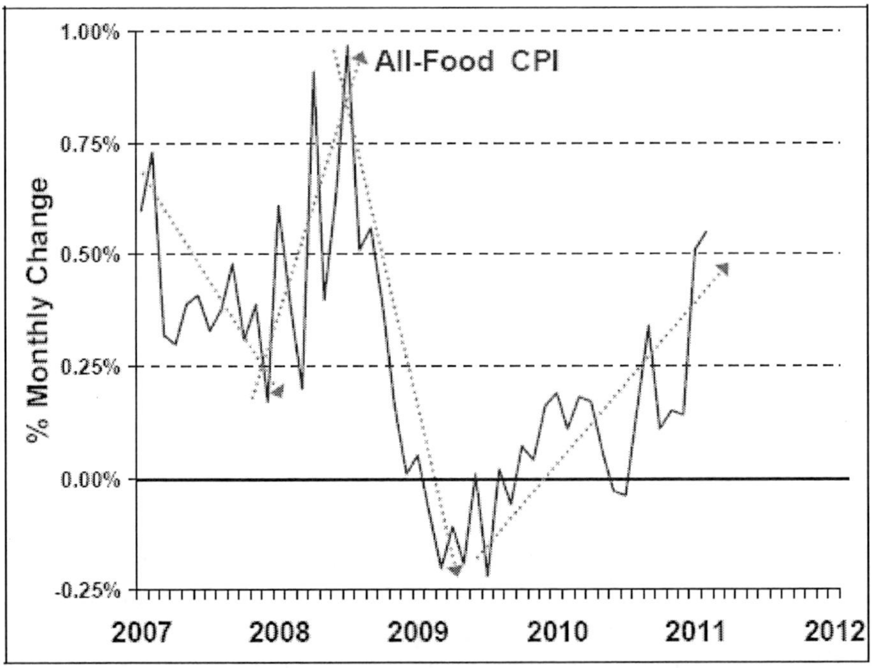


Source: Data, adjusted for seasonality, are from the Department of Labor, BLS.
Notes: The percent change is calculated from the CPI for successive months. Multiply any given month's value by 12 to approximate the annual inflation rate experienced during that particular month, without compounding.

Figure 8. Monthly Retail Food Price Inflation Trended Down in 2007, Spiked Sharply Higher in Early 2008, Plummeted into 2009, and Has Trended Up Since.

Month-to-month retail food price declines continued into 2009 even though farm prices had stabilized in early 2009. This is because food processors and retailers are traditionally slow to pass on price decreases that they experience at the wholesale level for several reasons, including substantial inherent operating risk associated with volatile markets.[13]

The same monthly all-food price inflation measures (also adjusted for seasonality) are presented in *Figure 9,* but for a longer time period and accompanied by their 11-month moving average (MA).[14] The MA series reveals a strong upward inflationary trend that began at the end of 2005 and persisted through June 2008. Since June 2008, the MA moved strongly downward until mid-2009 before reversing. Retail food prices were clearly responding to the deflationary pressures associated with the collapse of U.S. and international commodity prices that occurred in mid-2008, as well as to the crisis that emerged in late 2008 in U.S. and global financial markets.

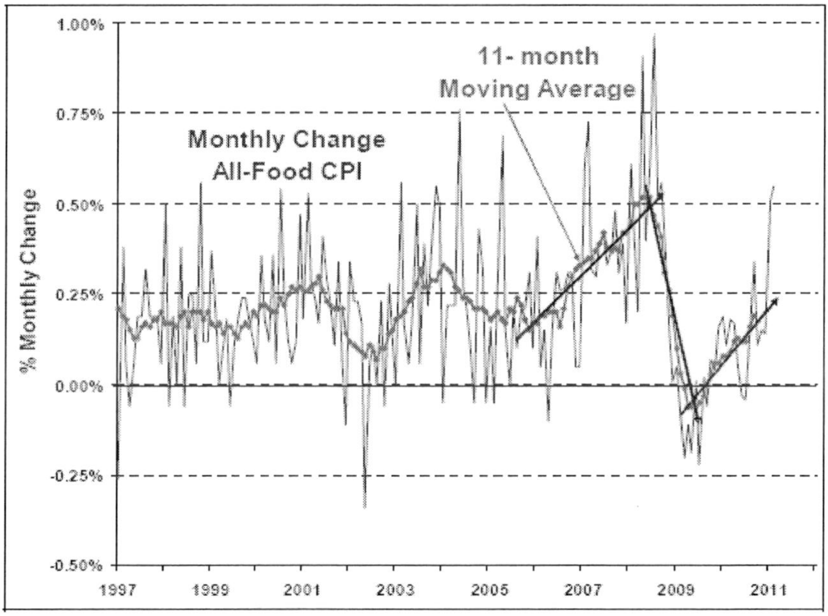


Source: Data, adjusted for seasonality, are from the Department of Labor, BLS.

Figure 9. Food Price Inflation Since 1997: Monthly Change vs. 11-Mo. Moving Ave.

## At-Home versus Away-from-Home Food Price Inflation

As shown earlier (*Figure 5*), at-home food prices are substantially more volatile than away-fromhome food prices (see also *Table 1*, where the at-home food price SD of 1.7% compares with a 1.0% SD for away-from-home food prices since 1983). This volatility is apparent, even when using a shorter time period (*Table 4* and *Figure 10*). It is not surprising, then, that at-home food prices made a steeper decline in 2009 and 2010, but are expected to make a sharper reversal in 2011 than either all-food or food-away-from-home.

When displayed in terms of monthly price changes, the pattern exhibited by at-home food price inflation (*Figure 11*) appears very similar to the pattern for all-food price inflation (*Figure 8*), although the at-home food price movements are more extreme. In contrast, monthly away-fromhome price inflation is much more stable. Note that both at-home and away-from-home monthly price inflation show a distinct downturn beginning in July 2008 and running into early 2009, followed by a steady recovery into 2011.

(historical data since 1997, with forecast for 2011)

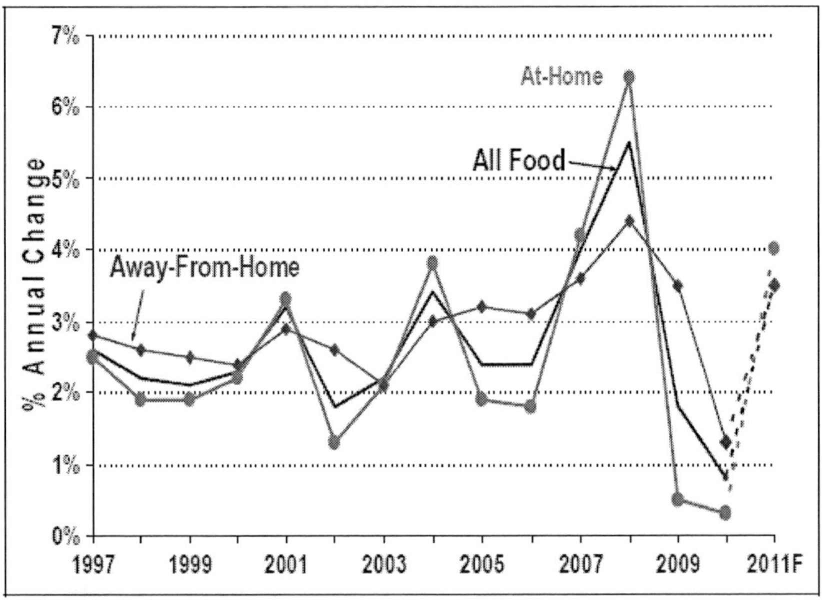


Source: See source info from Table 4.

Figure 10. Annual Food Price Inflation for All, At-Home, and Away-from-Home CPI.

## Price Inflation by Major Food Categories

The demand-side influences of income growth (and decline) and the global financial crisis that emerged in late 2008 have already been discussed briefly. On the supply side, food price inflation is the result of dynamic forces that occur both at the farm where the raw agricultural ingredients for retail food items are produced, and along the marketing chain as the farm output is transformed and moved to the retail customer. An array of costs are layered on top of the price of the raw agricultural commodity, including handling, transportation, storage, and processing, as well as the insurance, financing, and advertising costs necessary to move the product to the retail customer. The relative importance of these marketing costs varies widely for different retail food products depending on the degree of processing and transformation (i.e., cleaning, packaging, shipping, advertising, etc.). As a result, economic forces such as higher energy costs or increased labor rates do not impact all food categories equally.

### *Annual Price Movements by Major Food Categories*

The relatively high food price inflation of 2007 and 2008 was not felt evenly across all food groups, but varied widely in terms of both the timing and the relative magnitude of inflation. In 2008, the inflation rate for at-home food was 6.4% (Table 5); however, only the "fruits and vegetables" category experienced a similar level of price inflation (6.2%). Several product categories experienced substantially higher inflation, including egg prices, which were up 14% in 2008 after having soared by 29% in 2007; fats and oils were up 13.8%, cereals and bakery products up 10.2%, snacks up 8.1%, and dairy products up 8%.

**Table 4. Annual Food Price Inflation Since 2006**

| Category | Weights | | Annual % Change | | | | |
|---|---|---|---|---|---|---|---|
| | | 2006 | 2007 | 2008 | 2009 | 2010 | 2011F |
| All-Items | na | 3.2 | 2.8 | 3.8 | -0.4 | 1.6 | 1.6 |
| All-Food | 100% | 2.4 | 4.0 | 5.5 | 1.8 | 0.8 | 3.0 to 4.0 |
| Food-at-Home | 55.8% | 1.7 | 4.2 | 6.4 | 0.5 | 0.3 | 3.5 to 4.5 |
| Food-Away-from-Home | 44.3% | 3.1 | 3.6 | 4.4 | 3.5 | 1.3 | 3.0 to 4.0 |

Source: Historical data (adjusted for seasonality) through 2010 are from BLS, Dept of Labor; 2011 forecasts are from ERS, USDA, as of March 25, 2011, at http://www.ers.usda.gov/Briefing/ CPIFoodAndExpenditures/Data/ cpiforecasts. htm. The all-items CPI forecasts for 2011 are from Global Insights, U.S. Economic Outlook, April 2011.

Notes: BLS data are as of April 2011 using 2005-2006 weights for U.S. City Average (CPI-U). Annual percent changes are calculated from annual average indexes.

In contrast, the broad price index of meats, poultry, and fish was up only 4.2%, and non-alcoholic beverages (including carbonated and non-carbonated drinks and juices) were up 4.3%.

(at-home vs. away-from-home)

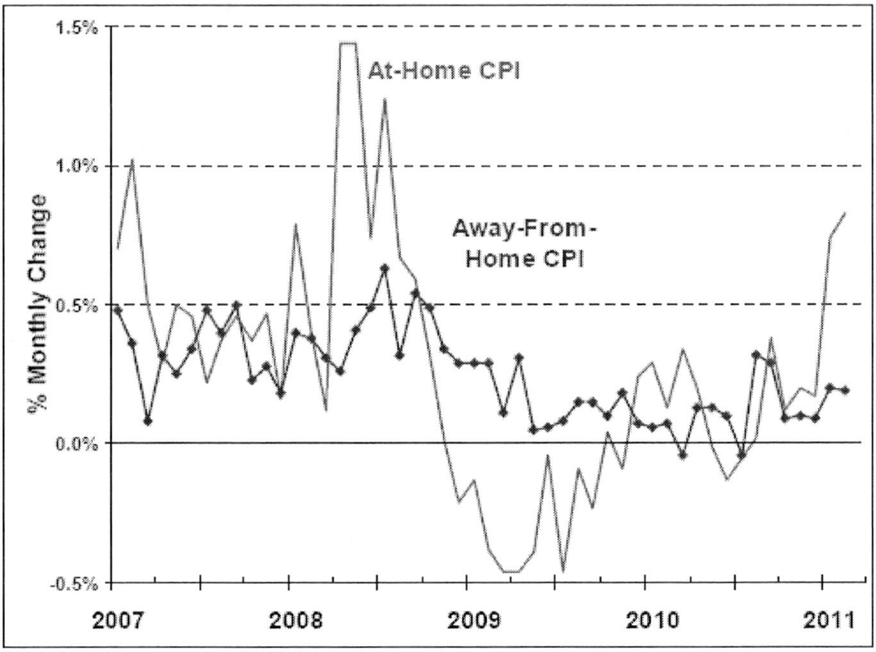


Source: Historical data (adjusted for seasonality) are from BLS, Dept of Labor.

Notes: The percent change is calculated from the CPI for successive months. Multiply any given month's value by 12 to approximate the annual inflation rate experienced during that particular month, without compounding.

Figure 11. Monthly Retail Food Price Inflation Since July 2007.

Similarly, the economic downturn sparked by the financial crisis of late 2008 led to sharply lower food-at-home inflation rates of 0.5% and 0.3% in 2009 and 2010; however, the price changes varied substantially across food groups. For example, milk prices fell 13.2% in 2009, but rose 3.6% in 2010. Egg prices fell 14.7% in 2009 then rose 1.5% in 2010. The price lag associated with the marketing chain resulted in price changes for more processed foods (e.g., cereal and bakery products; non-alcoholic beverages; processed fruits and vegetables; and other foods) declining in 2010, whereas less processed foods (e.g., meats, poultry, and fish; fruits and vegetables; and eggs) showed the most drop off in 2009.

### Table 5. The Food-at-Home CPI by Category Since 2006

| | Weights[a] | | | Annual Percent Change | | | | |
|---|---|---|---|---|---|---|---|---|
| Category | % | % | 2006 | 2007 | 2008 | 2009 | 2010 | 2011F |
| Food at Home | 100% | | 1.7 | 4.2 | 6.4 | 0.5 | 0.3 | 3.5-4.5 |
| 1-Cereal & Bakery Products | 13.9% | | 1.9 | 4.4 | 10.2 | 3.2 | -0.8 | 3.5 to 4.5 |
| Cereals and products[b] | | 4.5% | 0.3 | 3.9 | 10.1 | 3.4 | -1.9 | Na |
| Bakery products[c] | | 9.4% | 2.6 | 4.5 | 10.3 | 3.0 | -0.4 | Na |
| 2-Meats; Poultry; & Fish | 22.0% | | 0.8 | 3.8 | 4.2 | 0.5 | 1.9 | 4.0 to 5.0 |
| Beef & veal | | 6.8% | 0.8 | 4.5 | 4.5 | -1.0 | 2.9 | 4.5 to 5.5 |
| Pork | | 4.2% | -0.3 | 2.0 | 2.3 | -2.0 | 4.7 | 6.0 to 7.0 |
| Poultry | | 4.1% | -1.8 | 5.2 | 5.0 | 1.7 | -0.1 | 2.5 to 3.5 |
| Fish & seafood | | 3.7% | 4.7 | 4.6 | 6.0 | 3.6 | 1.1 | 4.5 to 5.5 |
| 3-Eggs | 1.3% | | 4.9 | 29.2 | 14.0 | -14.7 | 1.5 | 4.5 to 5.5 |
| 4-Dairy & Products | 10.7% | | -0.6 | 7.4 | 8.0 | -6.4 | 1.1 | 4.5 to 5.5 |
| Milk | | 3.8% | -1.2 | 11.7 | 6.0 | -13.2 | 3.6 | Na |
| Cheese | | 3.6% | -1.4 | 5.9 | 12.1 | -5.2 | 0.7 | Na |
| Ice Cream | | 1.8% | 0.9 | 2.3 | 5.1 | 2.0 | -0.8 | Na |
| Other | | 2.0% | 0.6 | 6.1 | 7.7 | -2.4 | -0.7 | Na |
| 5-Fruits & Vegetables | 14.7% | | 4.8 | 3.8 | 6.2 | -2.1 | 0.2 | 3.0 to 4.0 |
| Fresh fruits | | 5.6% | 6.0 | 4.5 | 4.8 | -6.1 | -0.6 | 3.0 to 4.0 |
| Fresh vegetables | | 5.6% | 4.6 | 3.2 | 5.6 | -3.4 | 2.0 | 4.0 to 5.0 |
| Processed fruits & veg. | | 3.5% | 2.9 | 3.6 | 9.5 | 6.6 | -1.3 | 3.0 to 4.0 |
| 6-Non-alcoholic Beverages | 11.8% | | 2.0 | 4.1 | 4.3 | 1.9 | -0.9 | 2.0 to 3.0 |
| Juices & non-alc. drinks | | 8.0% | 2.3 | 4.2 | 4.4 | 2.6 | -1.4 | Na |
| Coffee, tea, & other | | 4.1% | 1.6 | 4.0 | 4.2 | 0.4 | 0.6 | Na |
| 7-Sugar & Sweets | 3.8% | | 3.8 | 3.1 | 5.5 | 5.6 | 2.2 | 2.5 to 3.5 |
| 8-Fats & Oils | 3.0% | | 0.2 | 2.9 | 13.8 | 2.3 | -0.3 | 5.0 to 6.0 |
| 9-Other Foods[d] | 18.7% | | 1.4 | 1.8 | 5.2 | 3.7 | -0.5 | 2.5 to 3.5 |
| Frozifreeze-dried foods | | 3.8% | 0.4 | 1.9 | 4.3 | 2.8 | -1.7 | Na |
| Snacks | | 3.8% | 1.5 | 2.0 | 8.1 | 6.7 | 1.6 | Na |

Source: Historical data (not adjusted for seasonality) for 2005 to 2010 are from BLS, Department of Labor, for the U.S. City Average (CPI-U). The 2011 forecasts are from ERS, USDA, as of March 25, 2011.

[a] Weights are "as a percent of total at-home food expenditures."

[b] Flour and prepared flour mixes, breakfast cereals, rice, pasta, and cornmeal.

[c] Bread, fresh biscuits, rolls, muffins, cakes, cupcakes, cookies, and other bakery products.

[d] Includes soups, spices, seasonings, condiments, sauces, baby food, and other miscellaneous foods.

In 2011, at-home food prices are forecast to rise strongly within a range of 3.5% to 4.5%. Meat products and fats and oils are expected to show the strongest price growth, while all food categories are projected up by at least 2.5%.

### *Monthly Price Movements by Major Food Categories*

Annual averages can cloud over substantial inter-year price movements. As a result, it is worthwhile to glance over the monthly price indexes for the past four years to get a better sense of the general pattern of retail food price movements across the various food groups. Monthly price indexes (*Figure 12*) for the four principal food groups—cereals and bakery products; meats (including beef, pork, poultry, and seafood); dairy products (including milk, cheese, ice cream, and other); and fruits and vegetables (including fresh as well as processed)—reveal very different patterns of price movement.[15]

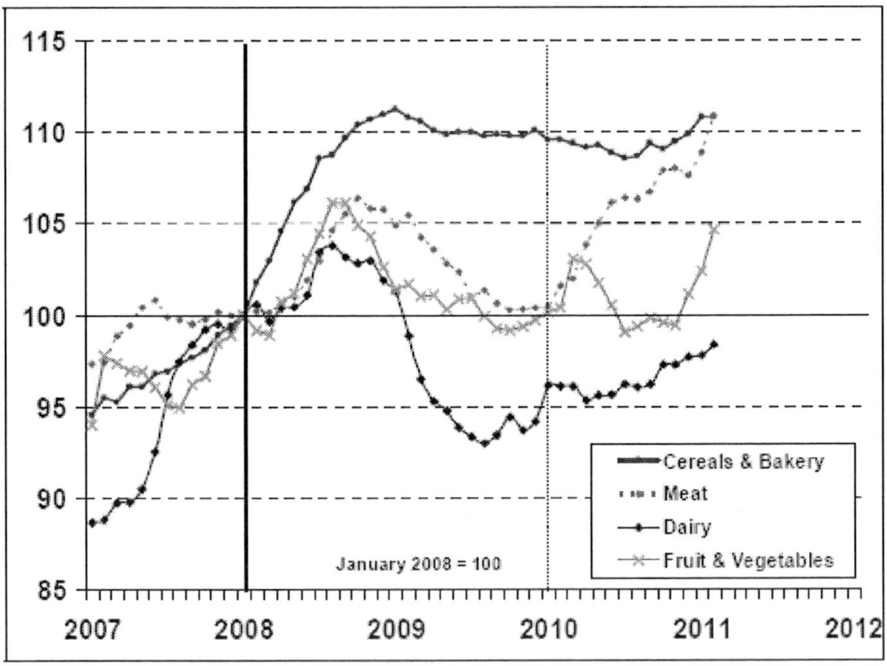


Source: Seasonally adjusted monthly CPI data, BLS, Department of Labor.

Figure 12. Monthly Retail Price Indexes: Various Major Food Groups.

The cereals and bakery product price index showed the strongest increase, rising nearly 18% between January 2007 and January 2009, but has been relatively stable since then. The dairy price index showed a strong rise through 2007 and into 2008, then declined slightly through the second half of 2008 before falling sharply in early 2009. Dairy prices have moved steadily upward since mid-2009 but have yet to return to their January 2008 level. The fruit and vegetable price index has shown considerable volatility, as a general upward pattern has been punctuated by significant deflationary movements during 2007, 2009, and 2010. The meat price index has also trended upward over this period, but with a sharp downturn in 2009 followed by an even sharper upturn since early 2010.

Perhaps the most dramatic and volatile of the individual foods price indexes has been eggs (*Figure 13*), which rose 35% from January 2007 to January 2008, then fell over 20% by July 2009. A year-over-year production decline from 2006 to 2007 coupled with strong exports tightened U.S. egg supplies and pushed prices sharply higher in 2007. Stronger egg production by mid-2008 coupled with the global economic crisis dampened prices starting in the later half of 2008. General economic growth has pulled egg prices upward steadily since mid-2009, but they remain well below their mid-2008 peak.

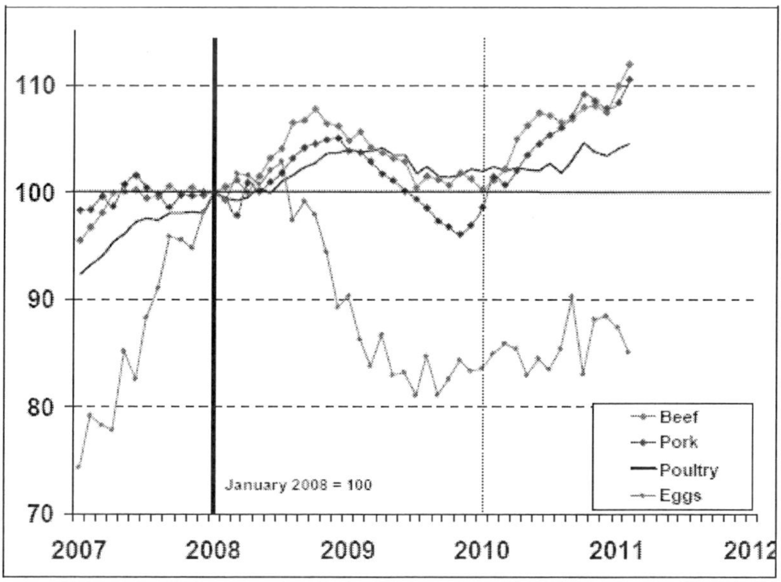


Source: Seasonally adjusted monthly CPI data, BLS, Department of Labor.

Figure 13. Monthly Retail Price Indexes: Beef, Pork, Poultry, and Eggs.

Beef and pork prices have shown considerable strength since early 2010 and are still following a strong upward trend in early 2011. Poultry prices have been more stable and have only ticked upward in the last half of 2010.

The components of the dairy group (*Figure 14*) followed distinctly different patterns, particularly the price index for fresh milk, which showed a sharp escalation in early 2007 (up 20% on the year), followed by a sharp drop-off in 2008, including a 22% fall from July 2008 to August 2009, before trending higher. The milk price pattern for the 2007-2009 period was very similar to the egg price pattern for that same period, and for the same principal reasons—initially tight supplies and expensive feed costs, followed by increased supplies and a sharp drop in prices and demand.

U.S. milk production expanded through 2007 and into 2008, while the global economic crisis weakened demand, especially from international markets. A resumption of U.S. and global economic growth have helped sustain price increases since late 2009. In contrast, highly processed ice cream showed a fairly steady upward rise from mid-2007 before slowing in early 2009, then growing sharply in late 2010 with the improving general economy.

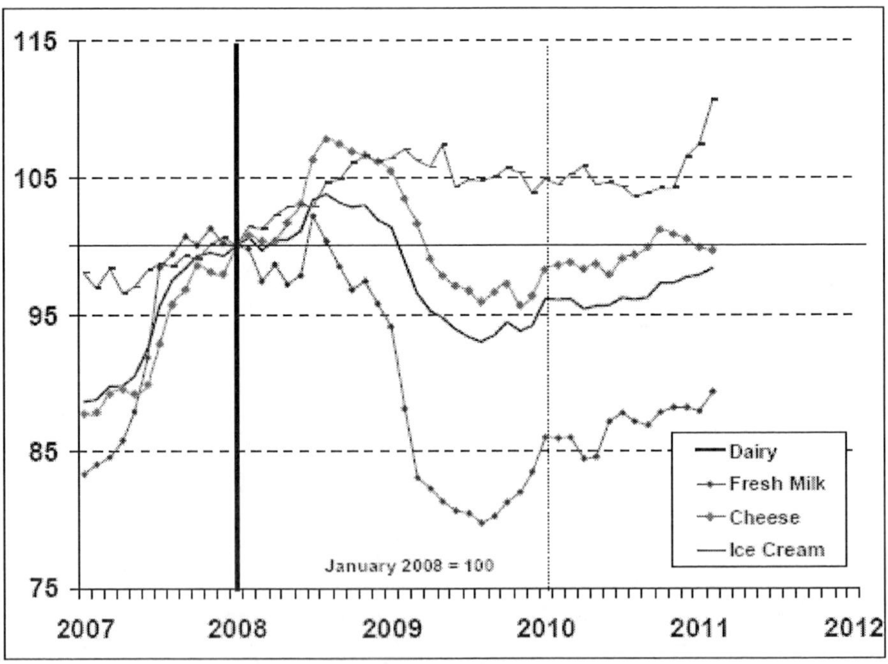


Source: Seasonally adjusted monthly CPI data, BLS, Department of Labor.

Figure 14. Monthly Retail Price Indexes: Dairy, Fresh Milk, Cheese, and Ice Cream.

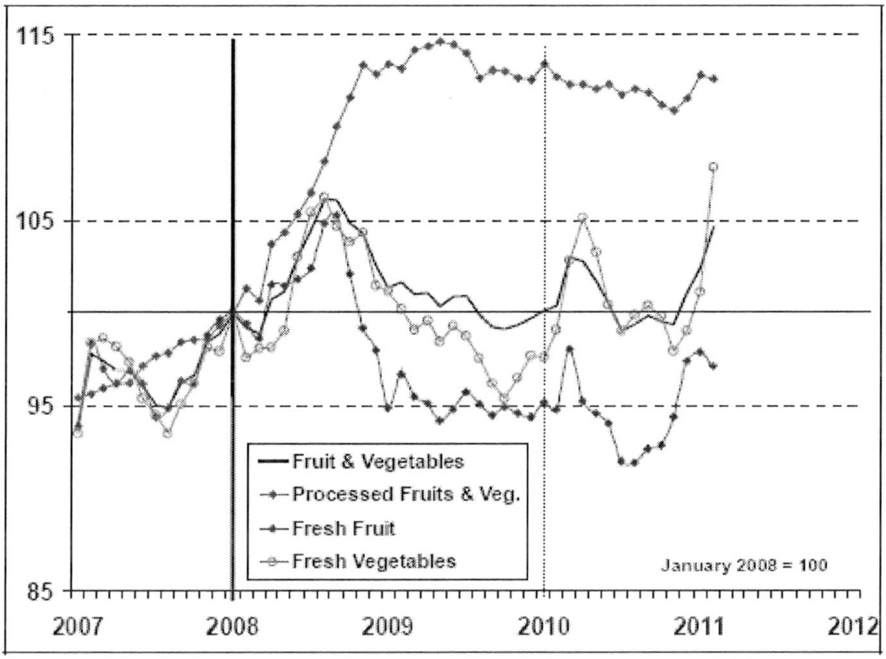


Source: Seasonally adjusted monthly CPI data, BLS, Department of Labor.

Figure 15. Monthly Retail Price Indexes: Fruits and Vegetables.

Similar to ice cream, the price index for processed fruits and vegetables (*Figure 15*) rose steadily through 2008, before leveling off, then ticking upward in late 2010. In contrast, the price indexes for fresh fruit and fresh vegetables exhibited volatile, slightly upward patterns into mid-2008 before declining through mid-2010. In late, 2010 the fresh fruit and vegetable indexes all showed a strong upward price movement into early 2011.

The price index for highly processed snacks (*Figure 16*) rose slowly in 2007, then accelerated upward during 2008 before falling back somewhat in 2009, then trending higher through 2010. The sugar and sweets price index had a similar pattern, although with a somewhat slower rise during 2008. The fats and oils price index rose rapidly during 2007 and during the first nine months of 2008, then fell back as the global market for oils became over-supplied, in part due to the fall-off in demand (related to the global financial crisis) in lesser-developed countries, where fats and oils are still treated as luxury goods. A resumption of global economic growth in 2010 has pulled the fats and oils price index upward since early 2010, with a sharp uptick in early 2011.

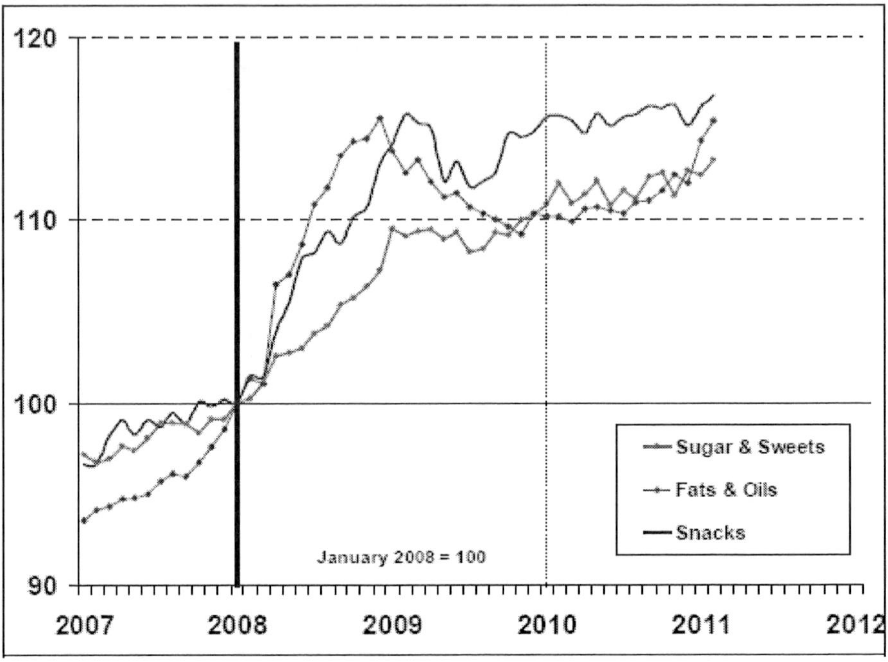


Source: Seasonally adjusted monthly CPI data, BLS, Department of Labor.

Figure 16. Monthly Retail Price Indexes: Sugar, Fat & Oils, and Snacks.

Similar to other highly processed food products, the prepared-food group (which includes frozen and freeze-dried prepared foods) and the carbonated beverages index both rose steadily through 2008 (*Figure 17*). However, both the prepared foods and carbonated beverages price indexes showed signs of leveling off in early 2009. Carbonated beverage prices have resumed their upward movement in 2010 with the global economic recovery. However, prepared foods continued a slow downward trend through 2010 as their greater dependence on the U.S. market and the slow U.S. economic recovery have kept demand in check. Coffee prices followed a similar, but more pronounced, pattern with a sharper rise in both 2008 and late 2010, and a more rapid descent through 2009.

In sum, evidence from recent years suggests that highly processed foods more consistently adhere to steady, stable upward price trends. In contrast, prices for less-processed retail food products— such as eggs, milk, and fresh fruits and vegetables—respond far more quickly to changes in both farm commodity prices and economic conditions and have followed farm prices downward in the early months of 2009, then upward sharply since late 2010.

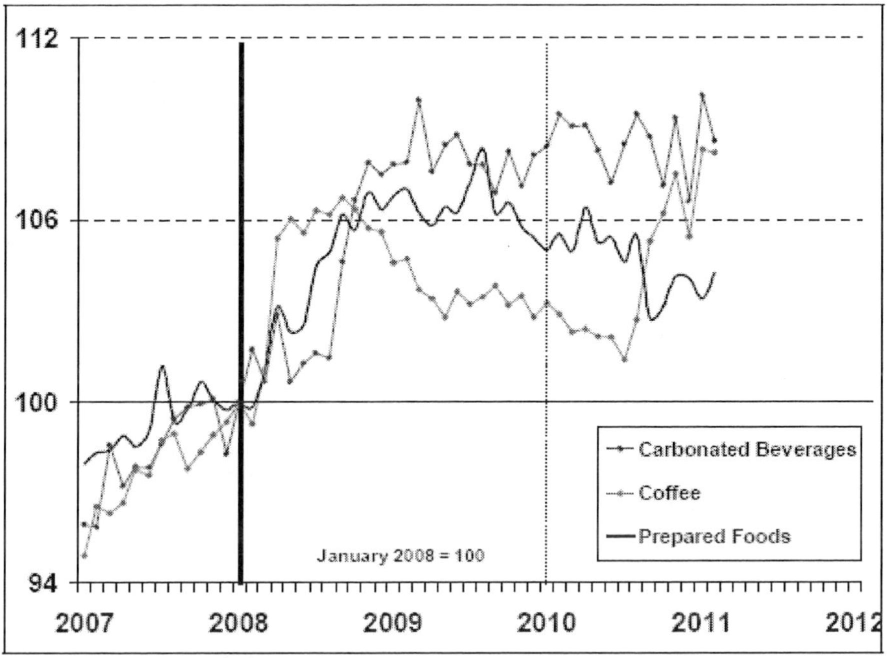


Source: Seasonally adjusted monthly CPI data, BLS, Department of Labor.

Figure 17. Monthly Retail Price Indexes: Coffee, Carbonated Beverages, and Prepared Foods.

## EFFECT OF HIGH PRICES

For a given level of income, higher prices mean lower effective purchasing power, since the same household budget will now acquire a smaller volume of products. As stated earlier in this report, lower-income consumers who spend a significant share of their household budget on food are likely to be impacted more severely by rising food prices, to be more responsive to price changes, and to be forced to make more difficult budgetary tradeoffs than high-income consumers with lower food budget shares.

The surge in agricultural commodity prices as well as the rise in costs of raw materials, energy, and transportation that persisted from mid-2005 through early 2008 translated into higher retail prices for food and other household products with all-food CPI averaging 5.5% in 2008. The negative aspects of high retail prices was magnified by the global financial crisis that emerged in 2008. The economic downturn manifested itself in a decline in household wealth due to sharply lower real estate values, tighter business and consumer credit, and rising unemployment numbers.

Although commodity prices peaked in early 2008 and began a steady decline through 2010, most retail prices were slow to reflect wholesale commodity price declines, and it was only in early 2009 that retail prices significantly retreated for most foods. This price deflationary trend persisted into 2010 and provided some budgetary relief for households with employed members.

However, surging unemployment numbers meant that many households were unable to take advantage of food price declines.

After a nearly two-year hiatus, commodity prices have resumed their upward surge since mid-2010. As a result, food price inflation is projected to average in the 3.5% to 4.5% range in 2011.

The effect of higher food prices is likely to be exacerbated by the recent high U.S. unemployment rate associated with the economic recession of 2008 and 2009. The U.S. unemployment rate averaged 9.3% in 2009 and 9.6% in 2010 after averaging 5.0% during the previous decade (1999 to 2008).

Many wages and salaries, as well as federal programs (including several domestic food assistance programs), are linked to price inflation through escalation clauses in order to retain their purchasing power. For households where income does not keep up with price inflation, declines in purchasing power are both real and immediate. However, even for households with escalation clauses that adjust incomes or benefits for price inflation, there is a time lag between the time the price inflation is measured and the time when the wage or program benefit is adjusted upward to compensate. As a result, for households with incomes or federal benefits linked to price inflation escalators, higher prices can cause a short-term decline in real purchasing power. This is most meaningful when prices are accelerating. When prices are falling, as during a deflationary period, consumers with fixed incomes realize gains in real income (provided that they are not subject to wage cuts or layoffs).

## Federal Spending for Domestic Food Assistance Programs

The U.S. Department of Agriculture (USDA) administers 15 domestic food and nutrition programs that provide a nutritional safety net for millions of low-income households, as well as schoolchildren and nutritionally vulnerable groups such as pregnant and/or lactating mothers.[16] The past decade has seen a tremendous expansion in use of USDA's food and nutrition assistance programs—federal expenditures totaled $94.8 billion in FY2010 and marked the 10th consecutive year in which food and nutrition assistance expenditures exceeded the previous historical record.[17] Since FY2004, expenditures for food and nutrition assistance have more than doubled.

The five largest food and nutrition assistance programs in FY2010 accounted for 96% of USDA's expenditures for food and nutrition assistance. Those programs are (1) the Supplemental Nutrition Assistance Program (SNAP), (2) the National School Lunch Program, (3) the Special Supplemental Nutrition Program for Women, Infants, and Children (WIC), (4) the Child and Adult Care Food Program, and (5) the School Breakfast Program. Each of these five major programs expanded, to varying degrees, during fiscal 2010.

A substantial portion of spending on these programs is in the form of entitlements (i.e., mandatory spending) whereby eligibility and participation rates govern outlays. For mandatory programs, food price inflation leads to more spending on domestic assistance efforts. Increasing prices encourage those who are eligible, but not participating, to enroll. They also translate directly (albeit with a time lag) into higher benefit payments and per-meal subsidies for "entitlement" programs in which benefits are indexed to food-price inflation. However, many of these programs also include discretionary components where outlays are determined through the annual appropriations process. Increasing prices places pressure on appropriators to provide more funding to support caseloads for "discretionary" programs like the WIC program.

The 2008-2009 global economic crisis—with its higher unemployment, income loss, and lower effective household purchasing power—following on the heels of higher retail prices, brought on higher participation rates and greater costs for domestic food aid programs. Although the U.S. economy resumed growth during 2010, unemployment ranks have been slow to follow. This is reflected in high SNAP participation levels, which hit an all-time high of 44.2 million (or 14.2% of the U.S. population) in January 2011 (the latest available information to date).[18] January 2011 also marked the 27th consecutive month that SNAP participation increased. SNAP monthly benefit costs have grown from $2.8 billion in January 2008 to $5.9 billion in January 2011, with average per-person monthly benefit spending rising from $100 to $133.

Other domestic food assistance programs also have seen increased participation (and costs). The number of lower-income children receiving free or reduced-price school lunches has risen from 31.0 million schoolchildren in

February 2008 to 31.8 million in January 2011.[19] Total outlays for the national school lunch, school breakfast, and special milk programs totaled $13.8 billion in FY2010.[20] WIC participation has grown from 8.6 million women, infants, and children in January 2008 to some 9 million in January 2011,[21] while the total cost was $6.7 billion in FY2010.[22]

### *Supplemental Nutrition Assistance Program (SNAP, Formerly Food Stamps)*

The SNAP, with nearly $68.3 billion in outlays in FY2010,[23] is the largest of the federally supported domestic food assistance programs. SNAP benefits normally are indexed annually (each October) for changes in the cost of USDA's least costly food plan, the "Thrifty Food Plan" (TFP). For a number of years and well into 2006, annual increases in the cost of the TFP typically ranged between 1.5% and 2.5%. However, starting in late 2006, food prices reflected in the cost of items in the TFP began to increase at a much faster rate. For example, basic benefits were increased by 4.6% in FY2007 and by 8.5% in October 2008. While these were substantial increases, they lagged by three months in reflecting rising food costs—they were (by law) based on prices from the immediately previous June. Thus there is a three-month gap between the calculation of the price inflation index in June and its use to adjust SNAP benefits in October.

In recognition of the lag in the inflation index for SNAP benefits, increased food needs, and reduced income, the 2009 American Recovery and Reinvestment Act (ARRA; P.L. 111-5) provided additional support for domestic food assistance programs: an estimated $11.5 billion for FY2009-FY2010 and $20.8 billion through FY2019.[24] SNAP was the primary recipient of this new money, most of which will be used to pay for added benefits, loosened eligibility standards, and administrative costs.

However, these increased SNAP benefits were reduced as part of P.L. 111-226 (a law providing funding for education jobs and Medicaid) and were further reduced by child nutrition reauthorization legislation (the Healthy, Hunger-Free Kids Act of 2010; P.L. 111-296).[25] As a result of these cuts, in November 2013 SNAP benefits will revert to what basic SNAP law directs (i.e., as calculated using annual food-price inflation).

### *Child Nutrition*

Federally supported child nutrition programs (e.g., the National School Lunch Program, the School Breakfast Program, the Special Milk Program, Child and Adult Care Food Program, and the Summer Food Service Program) and initiatives reach almost 32 million children. In FY2010, federal spending on these programs totaled nearly $17 billion, the second-largest federal commitment to domestic food assistance.[26] The basic goals of federal child nutrition programs are to improve children's nutrition, increase lower-income children's access to nutritious meals and snacks, and help support the agricultural economy.

Federal payments for meals and snacks served to children now range as high as $2.80 per meal, including the value of USDA commodity donations. Cash per-meal payments are indexed every July to food-price changes reflected in the food-away-from-home component of the CPI over the 12-month period ending each May. Commodity support (now some 21 cents per meal) also is indexed annually based on the Bureau of Labor Statistics' Producer Price Index for five major food components (cereal and bakery products, meats, poultry and fish, dairy products, processed fruits and vegetables, and fats and oils).

On December 13, 2010, Congress enacted the most sweeping changes in child nutrition and WIC programs since the 1970s.[27] The Healthy, Hunger-Free Kids Act of 2010 (P.L. 111-296) made substantial changes in child nutrition and WIC programs (most importantly, increasing federal financing for school lunches) that were estimated to cost just about $4.5 billion over 10 years. However, the act included spending reductions achieved by reducing future benefits under SNAP to offset the act's costs, and dropped authority for the Agriculture Department to bar certain foods from the WIC program.

### *The WIC Program*

Unlike the SNAP and child nutrition programs, which receive mandatory funding, the WIC program is funded from discretionary sources. Spending depends on annual appropriations, based largely on estimates of participation and the cost of the food packages that are purchased with WIC vouchers. In FY2010, over $7.2 billion was spent on WIC including $4.5 billion in food costs and $1.9 billion in nutrition service and administrative costs. The average monthly food cost per participant was $43.31.

The value of benefits is not indexed, per se. Rather, WIC vouchers are redeemable at whatever the participating retailer charges for the items covered by the vouchers, which differ according to the type of recipient (e.g., pregnant mother, infant, child). As a result, the cost of WIC vouchers reflect food price changes without the time lag built into other inflation-indexed nutrition programs. Just as important, WIC vouchers are highly specific as to the food items they cover and have a relatively heavy emphasis on certain types of food—for example, dairy items and infant formula are major components.

In recent years, the cost of WIC food vouchers has varied a great deal, largely because of changes in dairy-related food prices. The average per-participant monthly cost of vouchers has ranged from $34.80 in FY2002 to $43.41 in FY2008. However, the annual percentage increase has been very small for some years (1% or less for FY2003, FY2005, and FY2006) and more substantial for other years (6.6% for FY2004 and 5.6% for FY2007). Most recently, monthly per-participant WIC food costs averaged just under $43.13 in January 2011. Given this significant volatility, it is difficult to produce specific estimates of the effect of food price inflation on WIC program costs.

Although WIC spending is discretionary, Congress has historically shown a willingness to appropriate whatever amounts are necessary to meet costs imposed by increased participation or food costs. In 2009, it provided a $400 million contingency reserve to meet unexpected costs in FY2009 and FY2010 as part of the ARRA. However, recent (April 2011) budget appropriation negotiations appear likely to include substantial cuts in discretionary WIC spending.[28]

### *Additional Commodity Assistance Programs*

USDA operates several additional food assistance programs targeting low-income or vulnerable populations. The Emergency Food Assistance Program (TEFAP) and meal service programs under the Older Americans Act (e.g., "meals-on-wheels" and meals served to seniors in congregate meal settings) provide key food assistance support for vulnerable groups. The Commodity Supplemental Food Program (CSFP) provides foods purchased by USDA to low-income infants and children up to age six, low-income pregnant and postpartum women, and to low-income seniors citizens. The Senior Farmers' Market Nutrition Program (SFMNP) provides coupons to low-income seniors that can be exchanged for fresh, nutritious, unprepared, locally-grown fruits, vegetables, and herbs at farmers' markets, roadside stands, and community-supported agriculture programs. Like the WIC program, these programs are discretionary, and rising need and higher food prices have placed pressure on appropriators to add to federal funding. In FY2010, $248 million was appropriated for these programs.[29]

## Foreign Food Aid

USDA's international activities are funded by discretionary appropriations (e.g., foreign food assistance under the Food for Peace Act (P.L. 480) and by using the borrowing authority of the CCC (e.g., export credit guarantees, market development programs, and export subsidies).[30] Because foreign food aid is a budget value and not a food volume, its effective "purchase power" is diminished by food price hikes without additional appropriations. Unlike some domestic nutrition programs, foreign food aid is not adjusted to account for changing costs.

Food aid usually takes the form of basic food grains such as wheat, sorghum, and corn, and vegetable oil—commodities critical to developing-country diets. Since there is very little value added for these commodities, shifts in prices translate directly into higher prices for food-insecure countries or reduced food aid contributions per dollar spent. Also, higher energy costs have increased shipping costs for both food purchases and food aid.

## End Notes

[1] Examples of food groups include meat, dairy products, bakery goods, fruits, or vegetables.

[2] For more information on statistical issues related to the measurement of price inflation, see CRS Report RL30074, The Consumer Price Index: A Brief Overview, by Brian W. Cashell.

[3] For a brief discussion of 1970s energy markets, see CRS Report R40187, U.S. Energy: Overview and Key Statistics, by Carl E. Behrens and Carol Glover. For a brief discussion of 1970s agricultural markets, see May Peters, Suchada Langley, and Paul Westcott, "Agricultural Commodity Price Spikes in the 1970s and 1990s," Amber Waves, ERS, USDA, March 2009, at http://www.ers.usda.gov/; and Pete Riley, "Global Grain Markets in 1996: Shades of 1972-74?" Agricultural Outlook, AO-233, ERS, USDA, September 1996, pp. 2-6.

[4] For more information, see CRS Report RS22705, Inflation: Core vs. Headline, by Marc Labonte.

[5] "Personal Income and Outlays: February 2011," News Release BEA 11-14, March 28, 2011. The estimates for 2010 total and per-capita DPI were $11,380 billion and $36,822, respectively. However, comparable food expenditure data for 2010 were not yet available as of April 2011.

[6] The DPI and DPI-food-share estimates are for 2007 from Table 7, Food Expenditure Tables, Food CPI, Prices and Expenditures Briefing Room, ERS, USDA, at http://www.ers.usda.gov/Briefing/CPIFoodAndExpenditures/Data/.

[7] CES data are calculated "per consumer unit" which is described as "similar to a household" by BLS.

[8] For a discussion of this issue, see "Food Away From Home," Diet Quality and Food Consumption Briefing Room, ERS, USDA, at http://www.ers.usda.gov /Briefing/ Diet Quality/.

[9] Hayden Stewart, Noel Blisard, Sanjib Bhuyan, and Rodolfo M. Nayga, Jr., The Demand for Food Away From Home: Full-Service or Fast Food? AER No. 829, ERS, January 2004.

[10] For a discussion of food insecurity in the United States, see Food Security in the United States Briefing Room, ERS, USDA, at http://www.ers.usda.gov/Briefing/FoodSecurity/.

[11] For more information on the factors behind the sharp run-up in global commodity prices in the first half of 2008, see CRS Report RL34474, High Agricultural Commodity Prices: What Are the Issues? by Randy Schnepf.

[12] ERS updates its food price forecast monthly at Food CPI and Expenditures Briefing Room, ERS, USDA, at http://www.ers.usda.gov/Briefing/CPIFoodAndExpenditures/ consumer priceindex.htm.

[13] These issues are discussed in more detail in CRS Report R40621, Farm-to-Food Price Dynamics, by Randy Schnepf.

[14] Moving averages are used to reveal underlying patterns or trends that can otherwise be hidden by a substantial amount of month-to-month variation in price movements.

[15] Note that these statistics (based on the change in monthly price indexes) differ from the statistics reported in Table 5, where the inflation rates are calculated using the difference from annual averages rather than monthly averages.

[16] For details on the individual programs, see "Programs and Services," Food and Nutrition Service, USDA, at http://www.fns.usda.gov/fns/services.htm. Also see CRS Report R40397, Child Nutrition and WIC Programs: A Brief Overview, by Joe RichardsonFor a discussion of mandatory and discretionary program funding see CRS Report R41475, Agriculture and Related Agencies: FY2011 Appropriations, coordinated by Jim Monke.

[17] The Food Assistance Landscape, FY2010 Annual Report, Economic Information Bulletin No. 6-8, ERS, USDA, at http://www.ers.usda.gov/Publications/EIB6-8/EIB6-8.pdf.

[18] USDA, Food and Nutrition Service (FNS), Supplemental Nutrition Assistance Program, "Monthly Data—National Level: October 2008 through January 2011," at http://www.fns.usda.gov/pd/34SNAPmonthly.htm.

[19] USDA, FNS, Program Data—Child Nutrition Tables, "National School Lunch: FY1969–FY2010," at http://www.fns.usda.gov/pd/slsummar.htm.

[20] USDA, FNS, Program Data—Child Nutrition Tables, "Federal Cost of School Food Programs: FY1969–FY2010," at http://www.fns.usda.gov/pd/cncosts.htm.

[21] USDA, FNS, WIC Program, "Monthly Data—National Level: October 2007–January 2011," at http://www.fns.usda.gov/pd/37WIC_Monthly.htm.

[22] USDA, FNS, WIC Program, "Annual Data—National Level: FY1974–FY2010," at http://www.fns.usda.gov/pd/wisummary.htm

[23] USDA, FNS, Supplemental Nutrition Assistance Program, "National Level: Annual Summary, FY69 through FY2010," at http://www.fns.usda.gov/pd/SNAPsummary.htm.

[24] For more information, see CRS Report R40160, Agriculture, Nutrition, and Rural Provisions in the American Recovery and Reinvestment Act (ARRA) of 2009, coordinated by Jim Monke.

[25] For more information see CRS Report R41374, Reducing SNAP (Food Stamp) Benefits Provided by the ARRA: P.L. 111-226 and P.L. 111-296, by Joe Richardson, Jim Monke, and Gene Falk.

[26] USDA, FNS, Program Data—Child Nutrition Tables, at http://www.fns.usda. gov/pd/ cnpmain.htm.

[27] For more information, see CRS Report R41354, Child Nutrition and WIC Reauthorization: Issues and Legislation in the 111th Congress, by Joe Richardson.

[28] For more information, see CRS Report R41475, Agriculture and Related Agencies: FY2011 Appropriations, coordinated by Jim Monke.

[29] USDA, FY2012 Budget, Explanatory Notes for Committee on Appropriation, Volume 2, February 2011.

[30] For more information, see CRS Report R41072, International Food Aid Programs: Background and Issues, by Melissa D. Ho and Charles E. Hanrahan.

In: Inflation and the Consumer Price Index ISBN: 978-1-61942-705-1
Editors: E. L. Green, A. N. Walker 

*Chapter 5*

# INFLATION-INDEXING ELEMENTS IN FEDERAL ENTITLEMENT PROGRAMS*

***Dawn Nuschler***

## SUMMARY

In recent months, various proposals have been discussed in the context of ways to reduce federal budget deficits. One of the proposals, for example, is the use of a different measure of consumer price change to index various provisions of federal programs, including cost-of-living adjustments (COLAs). For example, under current law, the Social Security COLA is based on the Consumer Price Index for Urban Wage Earners and Clerical Workers (CPI-W). Under the proposal, the Social Security COLA would be based instead on the Chained Consumer Price Index for All Urban Consumers (Chained CPI-U or C-CPI-U). Because the goal of the Chained CPI-U is to better reflect how consumers change their buying habits in response to changes in prices, supporters of the proposal argue that it is a more accurate measure for computing COLAs and making other automatic program adjustments. Because the Chained CPI-U typically has risen more slowly than either the CPI-W or the "regular" CPI-U, however, opponents view the proposal as a backdoor way of reducing benefits. Some observers point out that the Chained CPI-U is published as a preliminary value that is subject to revision over a

* This is an edited, reformatted and augmented version of a Congressional Research Service publication, CRS Report for Congress R42000, from www.crs.gov, dated September 13, 2011.

period of more than two years, and that it may not accurately reflect the cost of living for certain groups, such as the elderly population.

The current discussion of a potential change in the way the Social Security COLA is computed raises questions about indexing in other federal entitlement programs. The purpose of this report is to identify key indexing elements in major federal entitlement programs under current law and present the information in a summary table. As shown here, indexing affects more than benefit levels paid to individuals through COLAs. Indexing also affects, for example, federal payments to providers and eligibility criteria for some programs. In addition, the report provides a brief description of the measures of consumer price change used to index various elements of these programs under current law, as well as the alternative measure of consumer price change (the Chained CPI-U) that has been proposed for computing Social Security COLAs and making inflation adjustments to other federal programs.

This report does not evaluate the best measure of consumer price change for making automatic inflation adjustments in federal entitlement programs. In addition, broader issues, such as the technical aspects of different measures of consumer price change, potential implications of using an alternative measure of price change to index various elements of major federal entitlement programs, and the indexing of other items (for example, the federal poverty threshold and parameters of the tax code) are beyond the scope of this report.

## INTRODUCTION

Recent deficit reduction commissions, including the National Commission on Fiscal Responsibility and Reform, have recommended using an alternative measure of consumer price change to make inflation adjustments to federal programs government-wide.[1] The proposal would change, for example, the way the Social Security cost-of-living adjustment (COLA) is computed, as well as COLAs under other federal programs. Rather than using the Consumer Price Index for Urban Wage Earners and Clerical Workers (CPI-W) to compute the Social Security COLA, the proposal calls for the Social Security COLA to be based on the Chained Consumer Price Index for All Urban Consumers (Chained CPI-U or C-CPI-U).[2]

In general, the goal of the Chained CPI-U is to more accurately reflect how consumers change their buying habits in response to changes in prices. The Chained CPI-U typically has risen more slowly than either the CPI-W or the "regular" CPI-U. Supporters of the proposal argue that the CPI-W overstates inflation and, therefore, overestimates how much money is needed for Social Security beneficiaries to maintain their standard of living. Opponents of the proposal, however, view using the Chained CPI-U to adjust Social Security benefits for inflation as a backdoor way of reducing benefits. They maintain that the market basket of goods and services purchased by the elderly is different from that of the general population around which the CPI is constructed. It is more heavily weighted with healthcare expenditures, which rise notably faster than the overall CPI, and thus they contend that the cost of living for the elderly is higher than reflected by the overall CPI. For this reason, some policymakers support using the experimental Consumer Price Index for the Elderly (CPI-E) to compute the Social Security COLA.[3]

The current discussion of a potential change in the way the Social Security COLA is computed has raised questions about indexing provisions in other federal entitlement programs. The purpose of this report is to identify key indexing provisions in major federal entitlement programs under current law and present the information in a summary table (see *Table 1*). The programs included in the table are based on the major mandatory spending programs/categories shown in *The Budget and Economic Outlook: An Update,* published by the Congressional Budget Office (CBO) in August 2011, with some modifications.[4] For example, the Congressional Research Service (CRS) identified specific *programs* within CBO *categories* (such as "child nutrition") and included additional programs, such as Railroad Retirement which is closely coordinated with the Social Security program. Although there are other federal entitlement programs with indexing provisions, the programs included in the table represent a majority of federal mandatory spending. *Table 1* is not intended to address or fully explain all of the indexing provisions within the laws and regulations governing these programs. Rather, it is an overview and a general guide.

The report also provides a description of the measures of consumer price change used to index various elements of these programs under current law and the measure of consumer price change that has been proposed for making inflation adjustments to a range of federal entitlement programs (the Chained CPI-U). It is not intended to evaluate the best measure of consumer price change for inflation adjustments within a particular program or programs. Similarly, broader issues, such as the technical aspects of different measures of consumer price change and the indexing of other items (for example, the federal poverty threshold and parameters of the tax code), are beyond the scope of this report.[5]

## CURRENT AND PROPOSED MEASURES OF CONSUMER PRICE CHANGE

The U.S. Bureau of Labor Statistics (BLS) publishes the CPI-W and the CPI-U whose month-tomonth fluctuations reflect changes in the prices faced by consumers. More specifically, the change in the indexes is the average change in the retail price of a market basket composed of more than 80,000 items purchased by consumers at outlets (e.g., grocery stores and gasoline stations) in 87 urban areas across the nation. Changes in the prices of items in each area are averaged together using weights that reflect the items' importance in the spending of the CPI-W population[6] and the CPI-U population.[7] The national CPI-W and CPI-U are calculated by combining the local area data for all items in the market basket to obtain a U.S. city average. The rates of change in consumer prices as measured by the national CPI-W for all items and national CPI-U for all items have differed only slightly over time.[8]

In addition to their use in calculating constant-dollar estimates of other economic indictors (e.g., earnings), the national CPI-W and CPI-U as well as indexes for specific goods and services (e.g., medical care) are used for inflation indexing by the federal government. The percentage change in the national CPI-W (all items) is the basis for determining the annual COLA of Social Security benefits and the national CPI-U (all items) is the basis for determining certain features of the Earned Income Tax Credit, for example.[9] In addition, the percentage change in the CPI-U for specific groups of items is used to inflation-adjust various features of other federal programs. For example, per-meal subsidies paid to schools under child nutrition programs are tied to changes in the CPI-U "food away from home" index (which is a combination of indexes for full-service meals and snacks, limited-service meals and snacks, food at employee sites and schools, food from vending machines and mobile vendors, and other food away from home).

As part of its ongoing efforts to develop an index that more accurately measures changes in the cost of living, BLS developed the Chained Consumer Price Index for All Urban Consumers (CCPI-U). The population of the C-CPI-U and CPI-U are the same. The prices used to calculate the C-CPI-U, CPI-U, and CPI-W are the same. However, the formula for calculating the C-CPI-U better accounts for the ability of consumers to maintain their standard of living in the face of an increase in prices overall by changing their spending pattern toward items whose prices have increased more slowly and away from items whose prices have increased more quickly. [10]

Although the C-CPI-U was first published in 2002, the modified measure has not replaced the CPI-U or CPI-W and no federal program has used the C-CPI-U to date. Some members of the public policy community interested in curtailing growth of the U.S. budget deficit have proposed switching inflation-indexed federal programs and income tax provisions to the C-CPI-U, however. Because the C-CPI-U typically has risen more slowly than either the CPI-W and CPI-U, changing the basis for indexation could substantially lower outlays and raise revenues. But, the proposal to switch from the CPI-W to the C-CPI-U has prompted concern in some quarters about the ability of Social Security beneficiaries to maintain their standard of living. Some have suggested instead changing to the experimental index for those at least 62 years old (CPI-E)[11] in the arguable belief that it better reflects the elderly population's experience with inflation (i.e., this population's above-average spending on health care services whose prices have increased faster than overall prices).[12]

## Policy Considerations

As shown in *Table 1*, inflation adjustments affect many features of federal entitlement programs. The most recognized effect of inflation adjustments is on benefit levels. For example, monthly cash benefits, such as Social Security and Supplemental Security Income benefits, increase when a COLA is paid. Other types of benefits are indexed as well. Non-cash benefits provided under the Supplemental Nutrition Assistance Program (SNAP),[13] for example, are indexed to reflect food-price inflation. Coverage amounts under Medicare's standard outpatient prescription drug benefit (Part D) are adjusted for inflation.

Inflation adjustments also affect entitlement programs in ways that are less well known, from federal payments to providers to program eligibility requirements. For example, when a Social Security COLA is paid, the amount of wages subject to the Social Security payroll tax increases.[14]

Indexing affects the number of Medicare beneficiaries subject to higher income-related Part B and Part D premiums, as well as the amount of Medicare payments to providers. In another example, indexing affects cost-sharing amounts paid by Medicaid beneficiaries for prescribed drugs and for non-emergency services provided in an emergency room. Per-meal subsidies paid to schools, for example, under the National School Lunch program are indexed. Finally, indexing affects eligibility criteria for some programs, including Medicaid and the child tax credit.

Generally, switching to the C-CPI-U to compute COLAs and index other elements of federal entitlement programs is considered as a cost-saving measure in an effort to reduce federal budget deficits. For example, CBO estimates that switching to the C-CPI-U to compute Social Security COLAs would reduce federal outlays by about $27 billion over five years (2012-2016) and by $112 billion over 10 years (2012-2021).[15]

If applied on a government-wide basis, however, switching to the C-CPI-U could increase program costs in some cases. Under Medicare, for example, cost-sharing amounts for outpatient drugs paid by low-income beneficiaries who receive subsidies under Part D are indexed annually to the CPI-U under current law. Because the Chained CPI-U grows more slowly than the CPI-U when consumer prices increase, indexing cost-sharing amounts to the Chained CPI-U would result in an increase in federal Medicare spending.

Similarly, consider the refundable portion of the child tax credit (referred to as the additional child tax credit or ACTC). Taxpayers must have earnings that exceed the refundability threshold to claim the ACTC. The lower the threshold, the greater the number of low-income taxpayers who become eligible for the refundable child tax credit. Indexing the refundability threshold to a lower inflation index would expand the availability of the refundable child tax credit.

A further consideration with respect to switching to a chain weighted CPI on a government-wide basis is that BLS has developed a chain weighted CPI for the CPI-U series only. BLS has not, for example, developed a chain weighted CPI for the CPI-W series, which is used to determine Social Security COLAs and COLAs under other federal programs. As such, some proposals call for using the Chained CPI-U in place of both the CPI-U and the CPI-W where those indexes are used for inflation adjustments under current law. It could be argued that it would be more consistent with current law to apply the chained CPI concept to the CPI-W series and use that index (rather than the Chained CPI-U) to compute Social Security COLAs and COLAs under other federal programs that use the CPI-W. Switching to a new measure of consumer price change (such as the Chained CPI-U) to index various provisions within complex federal programs would require careful consideration with respect to implementation to avoid inconsistencies within and across federal programs.

As CBO points out, another consideration with switching to the Chained CPI-U to compute COLAs and index other provisions of federal entitlement programs is that BLS publishes the index initially as a preliminary value and then revises it over a period of more than two years. As a result, federal programs would be indexed to a preliminary estimate of the Chained CPI-U that is subject to estimation error. CBO further points out that the Chained CPI-U "may understate growth in the cost of living for some groups, such as older people."[16]

**Table 1. Key Inflation-Indexing Elements in Major Federal Entitlement Programs**

| | Application of Index | Brief Description of Index | Rationale for Using a Particular Index (If Known) |
|---|---|---|---|
| | | Social Security[a] | |
| Are Benefits Indexed? | Social Security benefits are indexed using an annual cost-of-living adjustment (COLA) based on the Consumer Price Index for Urban Wage Earners and Clerical Workers (CPI-W). | The CPI-W, which is published by the U.S. Department of Labor's Bureau of Labor Statistics, is based on retail market prices for more than 80,000 items collected in 87 urban areas across the United States.<br>It is based on the purchasing patterns of individuals in the population who earn more than half of their income from clerical or wage occupations and were employed at least 37 weeks in the previous year. The CPI-W population represents about 32% of the total non-institutional population.<br>Before 1978, the CPI-W was the only CPI published.[b]<br>Information on the CPI-W is available at http://www.bls.gov/cpi/. | In 1972, Congress enacted legislation providing for automatic cost-of-living increases, beginning in January 1975 (P.L. 92-336).[c] Before the 1972 law, benefits were increased by Congress on an ad-hoc basis.<br>The legislative history indicates that some policymakers supported automatic increases to avoid the substantial time lags between benefit increases that had occurred in the past. Others believed that automatic increases tied to the increase in consumer prices would alleviate the persistent political pressure to increase benefits. Moreover, they believed that linking benefit increases to the change in consumer prices would result in smaller benefit increases compared to what Congress would enact on an ad-hoc basis.[d] |
| Other Major Indexing Provisions | The Social Security COLA triggers other changes in the Social Security program. For years in which a COLA is payable | The national average wage indexing series is determined by the Social Security Administration. The AWI reflects the | |

**Table 1. (Continued)**

| | Application of Index | Brief Description of Index | Rationale for Using a Particular Index (If Known) |
|---|---|---|---|
| | (i.e., there is an increase in the CPI-W over the measuring period), the Social Security taxable wage base and the exempt amounts under the Social Security retirement earnings test (RET) are adjusted according to the Average Wage Index (AWI). In addition, the substantial gainful activity (SGA) amount for blind disabled beneficiaries, which is tied to the RET, is adjusted according to the AWI.<br>Although not triggered by the Social Security COLA, the SGA amount for non-blind disabled beneficiaries is adjusted according to the AWI.<br>With respect to the computation of initial monthly benefits, elements of the benefit formula (the bend points) and workers' earnings histories (through age 60) are adjusted according to the AWI.<br>(Note: The income thresholds that determine whether a beneficiary must pay federal income taxes on part of his/her Social Security benefits are not indexed.) | average amount of total wages for each year after 1950, including wages in non-covered employment and wages in covered employment in excess of the Social Security taxable wage base. (A detailed definition of the AWI can be found in Title 20, Chapter III, section 404.211(c) of the Code of Federal Regulations.)[e] | |
| | | Medicare | |
| Are Benefits Indexed? | Some Medicare benefits are indexed annually to the Consumer Price Index for All Urban Consumers (CPI-U), such as the initial and catastrophic coverage | The CPI-U, which is published by the U.S. Department of Labor's Bureau of Labor Statistics, is based on retail market prices for more than 80,000 items collected in | |

| | Application of Index | Brief Description of Index | Rationale for Using a Particular Index (If Known) |
|---|---|---|---|
| | amounts under the standard outpatient prescription drug benefit (Part D). | 87 urban areas across the United States.<br>It is based on the purchasing patterns of all urban consumers and covers about 87% of the population.<br>Beginning in 1978, the CPI-U was introduced so that a broader share of the population would be included in estimates of changes in the price level (as compared with the CPI-W).[f]<br>Information on the CPI-U and its various components is available at http://www.bls.gov/ cpi/. | |
| Are Premiums Paid by Beneficiaries Indexed? | Generally, income thresholds used for the definition of high-income thresholds for higher Part B and Part D premiums are indexed annually based on the CPI-U. However, between 2010 and 2019, the thresholds are fixed; indexing is scheduled to resume in 2020. | | |
| Are Cost-Sharing Amounts Paid by Beneficiaries Indexed? | Cost-sharing amounts for outpatient drugs paid by low-income beneficiaries receiving subsidies under Part D are also indexed annually to the CPI-U. | | |
| Other Major Indexing Provisions | Provider payment amounts are also indexed.<br>For detailed information, see CRS Report RL30526, Medicare Payment Policies, Medicare Payment Policies. | | |
| | | Medicaid | |
| Are Eligibility Criteria Indexed? | Indexing using the CPI-U applies to eligibility for long-term care services for persons with home equity interest below $500K (up | See description of CPI-U under Medicare. | |

**Table 1. (Continued)**

| | Application of Index | Brief Description of Index | Rationale for Using a Particular Index (If Known) |
|---|---|---|---|
| | to $750K at state option). At state option, indexing using the CPI-U applies to eligibility for families that meet the financial requirements of former states' AFDC cash assistance programs. | | |
| | Indexing using the CPI-U, Medical Care Component, applies to traditional cost-sharing maximums, as well as selected components of alternative cost-sharing established under the Deficit Reduction Act (DRA) of 2005; the applicable DRA components include cost-sharing for prescribed drugs and for non-emergency services provided in an emergency room. | The Medical Care Component of the CPI-U covers the part of healthcare commodities, services, and health insurance premiums that consumers pay for "out of pocket." Source: BLS Handbook of Methods, Chapter 17, The Consumer Price Index, page 26, at http://www.bls.gov/opub/hom/pdf/homch17.pdf. | |
| Other Major Indexing Provisions | States are required to make "disproportional share hospital" (DSH) adjustments to the payment rates of hospitals treating large numbers of low-income and Medicaid beneficiaries. State-specific federal allotments are available for such payments. Beginning in FY2003 through FY2013, indexing using the CPI-U must apply to the federal DSH allotments. | See description of CPI-U under Medicare. | |
| | Supplemental Security Income (SSI) | | |
| Are Benefits Indexed? | The Social Security COLA, which is based on the CPI-W, triggers an increase in SSI benefits. SSI benefits are increased by the same percentage as. | See description of CPI-W under Social Security. | |

| | Application of Index | Brief Description of Index | Rationale for Using a Particular Index (If Known) |
|---|---|---|---|
| | | the Social Security COLA | |
| Other Major Indexing Provisions | The Social Security COLA, which is based on the CPI-W, triggers an increase in the earned income exclusion for students who receive SSI benefits.<br>The amount of the exclusion is increased by the same percentage as the Social Security COLA. | See description of CPI-W under Social Security. | |
| | (The countable resource limits for SSI eligibility ($2,000 for an individual and $3,000 for a couple) are not indexed and have been at the current levels since 1989.) | | |
| | | Earned Income Tax Credit | |
| Are Benefits Indexed? | Certain parameters used to calculate the credit are indexed to the CPI-U: maximum income level; phase-out income level (unmarried and married); and disqualifying investment income level. | See description of CPI-U under Medicare. | |
| Other Major Indexing Provisions | Not applicable.<br>However, many other tax provisions that are indexed use the CPI-U. | | |
| | Child Tax Credit (Refundable Portion) | | |
| Are Benefits Indexed? | The $1,000 per child value of the credit is NOT indexed to inflation, although the parameter that is indexed, the refundability threshold, can have an impact on the final value of the credit for certain low-income taxpayers. | | |
| Other Major Indexing Provisions | From 2001-2007, the refundability threshold used to calculate the refundable portion of the child tax credit (sometimes | See description of CPI-U under Medicare. | |

**Table 1. (Continued)**

| | Application of Index | Brief Description of Index | Rationale for Using a Particular Index (If Known) |
|---|---|---|---|
| | referred to as the additional child tax credit or the ACTC) was indexed to the CPI-U. From 2008-2012, the threshold was not indexed for inflation. After 2012, if only the EGTRRA modifications to the child tax credit are extended, the refundability threshold will again be indexed to inflation. The inflation adjustment for a given tax year is calculated as the amount by which the CPI-U for the preceding year exceeds the CPI-U in 2000. The inflation adjusted refundability threshold is then rounded to the nearest multiple of $50. | | |
| | UnemploymentCompensation | | |
| Are Benefits Indexed? | Unemployment compensation is indexed in 33states, as well as the District of Columbia, Puerto Rico and the Virgin Islands, based on the Average Weekly Wage in covered employment. | Benefits are indexed to Average Weekly Wages in the state, for employees who are covered by the unemployment insurance program. The Average Weekly Wage (AWW) is determined by calculation set by each state's law. | Indexing is used in states where unemployment compensation is intended to replace a specific percentage of wages. Most states link the maximum weekly benefit amount to a percentage of the average weekly wage. |
| Other Major Indexing Provisions | Sixteen states and the Virgin Islands index the tax base of state taxes collected under the authority of the State Unemployment Tax Acts (SUTA). Most of these states automatically adjust the tax base according to the state Average Annual Wage. A few states index to the Average Weekly Wage. | In most states that index the taxable wage base, the tax base is indexed to the Average Annual Wage (AAW) in the state. State law determines the methodology and exact period of time to be used to calculate each state's AAW. The AAW is computed variously in the states as the sum of wages over preceding calendar year, the sum of wages for | The intent is for the tax base to increase taxes in line with wage growth in the state and growth in the average weekly benefit amount. |

| | Application of Index | Brief Description of Index | Rationale for Using a Particular Index (If Known) |
|---|---|---|---|
| | (Note: Federal taxes collected under the authority of the Federal Unemployment Tax Act (FUTA) are not indexed.) | 12 months ending March 31, the sum of wages for 12 months ending June 30, or the sum of wages of the previous 12 months ending 6 months before effective date. | |
| Supplemental Nutrition Assistance Program (SNAP, Formerly the Food Stamp Program) | | | |
| Are Benefits Indexed? | SNAP benefits are indexed to reflect food-price inflation.<br>Normally, SNAP benefits are indexed annually to the cost of the Thrifty Food Plan, which is a market basket of food determined to be minimally adequate to a household's needs. However, under the American Recovery and Reinvestment Act (ARRA; P.L. 111-5), SNAP allotments have been increased temporarily to 113.6% of the June 2008 Thrifty Food Plan amounts. This increase expires on November 1, 2013, as P.L. 111-226 and P.L. 111-296 amended this ARRA provision. | Figures for the cost of U.S. Department of Agriculture food plans are calculated and published by the Agriculture Department's Center on Nutrition Policy and Promotion. | |
| Other Major Indexing Provisions | Income eligibility standards are tied to changes in the federal poverty income guidelines, which are indexed annually based on the CPI-U. The federal poverty income guidelines are issued by the U.S. Department of Health and Human Services.<br>Limits on liquid assets that eligible households may hold are indexed annually based on the CPI-U.<br>Other aspects of this program are indexed, but | See description of CPI-U under Medicare. | |

**Table 1. (Continued)**

| | Application of Index | Brief Description of Index | Rationale for Using a Particular Index (If Known) |
|---|---|---|---|
| | indexing is not at the individual benefit level for those aspects. Rather, those examples affect the magnitude of funding at a nationwide or state level. | | |
| Child Nutrition Programs (Including School Meal Programs, Assistance for Child Care and Other Outside-of-School Programs) | | | |
| Are Benefits Indexed? | Per-meal subsidies paid to providers (e.g., schools and child care centers) are indexed annually based on the CPI-U, Food Away from Home Component. For family child care homes, the annual indexing is based on the CPI-U, Food at Home Component. | The Food Away from Home Component of the CPI-U covers the following categories: full service meals and snacks; limited service meals and snacks; food at employee sites and schools; food from vending machines and mobile vendors; and other food away from home.<br>Source: BLS Handbook of Methods, Chapter 17, The Consumer Price Index, Appendix 2, page 3, available at http://www.bls.gov/opub/hom/ pdf/homch17.pdf. (For a detailed listing of items included in the Food at Home Component of the CPI-U, see Appendix 2, pages 1-3, of the BLS document.) | |
| Other Major Indexing Provisions | Income eligibility standards for free and reduced-price meals to lower-income children are tied to changes in the federal poverty income guidelines, which are indexed annually based on the CPI-U. The federal poverty income guidelines are issued by the U.S. Department of Health and Human Services. | See description of CPI-U under Medicare. | |

| | Application of Index | Brief Description of Index | Rationale for Using a Particular Index (If Known) |
|---|---|---|---|
| | Other aspects of these programs are indexed, but indexing is not at the individual benefit level for those aspects. Rather, those examples affect the magnitude of funding at a nationwide or state level. | | |
| | Civil Service Retirement System (CSRS)[g] | | |
| Are Benefits Indexed? | Benefits are indexed using an annual COLA based on the CPI-W. The program uses the same measuring period and formula for computing the COLA as the Social Security program.<br>All CSRS retirees and survivors receive COLAs. | See description of CPI-W under Social Security. | |
| Other Major Indexing Provisions | Not applicable. | | |
| | Federal Employees Retirement System (FERS)[h] | | |
| Are Benefits Indexed? | Benefits are indexed using an annual COLA based on the CPI-W. All COLAs paid under FERS are limited if the rate of inflation exceeds 2.0%. Nondisabled retirees under age 62 do not receive COLAs.<br>Survivors and disabled retirees are eligible for COLAs regardless of age. | See description of CPI-W under Social Security. | |
| Other Major Indexing Provisions | Not applicable. | | |
| | | Military Retirement | |
| Are Benefits Indexed? | Benefits are indexed using an annual COLA based on the CPI-W. The program uses the same measuring period and formula for computing the COLA as the Social Security program. | See description of CPI-W under Social Security. | |

**Table 1. (Continued)**

| | Application of Index | Brief Description of Index | Rationale for Using a Particular Index (If Known) |
|---|---|---|---|
| Other Major Indexing Provisions | Not applicable. | | |
| | Veterans Disability Compensation | | |
| Are Benefits Indexed? | Benefits are not indexed automatically. Legislation is passed each year providing a COLA equal to the Social Security COLA, which is based on the CPI-W.By law, any increase for 1998-2013 is limited to the Social Security COLA | See description of CPI-W under Social Security. | |
| Other Major Indexing Provisions | Not applicable | | |
| | | Veterans Pensions | |
| Are Benefits Indexed? | The Social Security COLA, which is based on the CPI-W, triggers an increase in veterans pension benefits. Benefits are increased by the same percentage as the Social Security COLA. | See description of CPI-W under Social Security. | |
| Other Major Indexing Provisions | Not applicable. | | |
| | Dependency and Indemnity Compensation | | |
| Are Benefits Indexed? | Benefits are not indexed automatically. Legislation is passed each year providing a COLA equal to the Social Security COLA, which is based on the CPI-W. By law, any increase for 1998-2013 is limited to the Social Security COLA. | See description of CPI-W under Social Security. | |
| Other Major Indexing Provisions | Not applicable. | | |
| | Railroad Retirement Board (RRB) | | |
| Are Benefits | The Social Security | See description of CPI-W | RRB and Social Security |

| | Application of Index | Brief Description of Index | Rationale for Using a Particular Index (If Known) |
|---|---|---|---|
| Indexed? | COLA, which is based on the CPI-W, triggers an increase in RRB benefits. Tier I benefits (which are equivalent to Social Security benefits) are increased by the same percentage as the Social Security COLA. Tier II benefits (which are equivalent to private pensions) are increased by 32.5% of the Social Security COLA. | under Social Security. | benefits are closely coordinated. |
| Other Major Indexing Provisions | With respect to the computation of initial monthly tier I benefits, elements of the benefit formula (the bend points) and workers' earnings histories (through age 60) are adjusted according to the Average Wage Index (AWI). | See description of AWI under Social Security. | |

Source: Table prepared by the Congressional Research Service. The table is not intended to address or fully explain all of the indexing elements within the laws and regulations governing these programs. Rather, it is an overview and a general guide.

Notes: The Temporary Assistance for Needy Families (TANF) block grant is not included in the table. The TANF block grant does not provide entitlements to individuals. The block grant is an entitlement to the states, but is legislatively fixed and not adjusted. TANF does have contingency funds, that increase grants to states if certain conditions are met. (Program Contact: Gene Falk, 7-7344, gfalk@crs.loc.gov) In addition, Foster Care, Adoption Assistance and Kinship Guardianship Assistance (Title IV-E of the Social Security Act) are not included in the table. Neither monthly benefits nor program eligibility are indexed. States have complete discretion to determine benefit levels. Federal rules govern program eligibility and they are mostly static. (Program Contact: Emilie Stoltzfus, 7-2324, estoltzfus@crs.loc.gov)

[a] For more information, see CRS Report 94-803, Social Security: Cost-of-Living Adjustments.

[b] CRS Report RL30074, The Consumer Price Index: A Brief Overview.

[c] Under P.L. 92- 336, benefits were increased automatically each January if the cost of living increased 3% or more over the measuring period. Under current law, benefits are increased automatically if there is an increase of at least 0.1% in the

CPI-W over the measuring period. If there is a less than 0.1% change in the CPI-W, benefits stay the same. For information on the Social Security COLA computation under current law, see CRS Report 94-803, Social Security: Cost-of-Living Adjustments.

[d] Indexation of Federal Programs, Senate Budget Committee, 97th Congress, 1st Session, May 1981, pp. 143-146.

[e] The 2011 Annual Report of the Board of Trustees of the Federal Old-Age and Survivors Insurance and Federal Disability Insurance Trust Funds, p. 208.

[f] CRS Report RL30074, The Consumer Price Index: A Brief Overview.

[g] For more information, see CRS Report 94-834, Cost-of-Living Adjustments for Federal Civil Service Annuities.

[h] Ibid.

## End Notes

[1] For example, see The Moment of Truth: Report of the National Commission on Fiscal Responsibility and Reform, December 1, 2010, available at http://www. fiscalcommission. gov/sites/fiscalcommission.gov/files/documents/TheMomentofTruth12_1_2010.pdf.

[2] The Consumer Price Index (CPI) and its various series are measures of consumer price change published by the U.S. Department of Labor, Bureau of Labor Statistics (BLS). For more information on the CPI, see the BLS website at http://www.bls.gov/cpi/.

[3] For information on the projected effects of using the C-CPI-U and the CPI-E to compute the Social Security COLA, see Social Security Administration, Office of the Chief Actuary, Memo to the Honorable Xavier Becerra, June 21, 2011, available at http://ssa.gov/ OACT/solvency/index.html.

[4] Specifically, see Table 1-4, CBO's Baseline Projections of Mandatory Spending, on pages 18-19. The CBO report is available at http://www.cbo.gov/ftpdocs/123xx/doc12316/08-24-BudgetEconUpdate.pdf.

[5] For related information, see Center for Retirement Research at Boston College, Implications of a "Chained" CPI, by Alicia H. Munnell and William M. Hisey, September 2011, available at http://crr.bc.edu/images/stories/Briefs/IB_11-12_508.pdf.

[6] The CPI-W population is composed of households for whom at least one-half of household income comes from wage earners in clerical, craft, and sales among other occupations with at least one worker employed for 37 or more weeks. It covers about 32% of the U.S. population. The CPI-W series began in 1921.

[7] In 1978, BLS initiated the CPI-U in order to cover more of the U.S. population. Households in the CPI-U, which covers about 87% of the population, include the CPI-W population plus households of salaried workers (e.g., professionals and managers), part-time workers, the self-employed, the unemployed, and households with no one in the labor force (e.g., retirees).

[8] For additional information, see CRS Report RL30074, The Consumer Price Index: A Brief Overview and U.S. Bureau of Labor Statistics, Handbook of Methods, Chapter 17. The Consumer Price Index, Washington, DC, June 2007, http://www.bls.gov/opub/ hom/pdf/homch17.pdf.

[9] In addition, different inflation measurement periods are used by various programs.

[10] For additional information on the C-CPI-U and the current policy debate, see CRS Report RL32293, The Chained Consumer Price Index: What Is It and Would It Be Appropriate for Cost-of-Living Adjustments?

[11] The 1987 amendments to the Older Americans Act of 1965 (P.L. 100-175) directed BLS to develop a consumer priceindex for the elderly members of the population.

[12] Congressional Budget Office, Using a Different Measure of Inflation for Indexing Federal Programs and the Tax Code, Economic and Budget Issue Brief, February 24, 2010; and CRS Report RS20060, A Separate Consumer Price Index for the Elderly?

[13] SNAP was formerly known as the Food Stamp Program.

[14] When a Social Security COLA is paid, the Social Security taxable wage base is increased based on average wage growth.

[15] Congressional Budget Office, Reducing the Deficit: Spending and Revenue Options, March 2011, pp. 58-59, available at http://www.cbo.gov/ftpdocs/120xx/doc12085/03-10-ReducingTheDeficit.pdf.

In: Inflation and the Consumer Price Index ISBN: 978-1-61942-705-1
Editors: E. L. Green, A. N. Walker 

*Chapter 6*

# A SEPARATE CONSUMER PRICE INDEX FOR THE ELDERLY?*

*Linda Levine*

## SUMMARY

The federal government, in an effort to protect the purchasing power of Social Security beneficiaries, indexes benefits to increases in the Consumer Price Index for Urban Wage Earners and Clerical Workers (CPI-W). Concern has periodically been expressed that the CPI-W may understate the impact of inflation on the elderly population and that it therefore may not be the most appropriate measure of inflation's impact on the elderly.

At the behest of Congress, the U.S. Bureau of Labor Statistics (BLS) developed an experimental price index to track changes in the cost of living for the population aged 62 and older. The average annual rate of change between December 1982 and December 2010 in the experimental consumer price index (CPI-E) for the elderly was 3.1%. Over the same period, the CPI-W rose by 2.9%. Methodological limitations in the experimental index may have contributed to this difference, however. Were BLS to construct an index that is more representative of the elderly population, there is no guarantee that the relationship between the new index and the CPI-W would be the same.

* This is an edited, reformatted and augmented version of a Congressional Research Service publication, CRS Report for Congress RS20060, from www.crs.gov, dated September 27, 2011.

Interest in the CPI-E most recently has emerged in response to deficit-reduction plans that recommend that inflation-indexed provisions in federal law be based on the Chained Consumer Price Index for All Urban Consumers (C-CPI-U). Because the C-CPI-U typically has risen more slowly than the CPI-W, this proposal has raised concern among those Social Security recipients who already believe they have not been fully compensated for increases in their cost of living. As a result, there has been discussion about switching instead from the CPI-W to the faster rising CPI-E with regard to Social Security indexation. This would offset the deficit-reduction effect of changing from the CPI-W to the C-CPI-U, however, if increases in the CPI-E or a new index for the elderly continue to outpace those in the other price indexes.

## INTRODUCTION

In an effort to protect the purchasing power of Social Security recipients, Congress in the early 1970s indexed benefit increases to the only consumer price index available at the time. The index to which Social Security benefits are linked became known as the Consumer Price Index for Urban Wage Earners and Clerical Workers (CPI-W) after the U.S. Bureau of Labor Statistics (BLS) began publishing the Consumer Price Index for All Urban Consumers (CPI-U) in 1978.[1]

Concern has periodically been expressed that the CPI-W may not accurately reflect the inflation experience of the elderly, who make up the majority of Social Security beneficiaries. It has been asserted that the elderly face a higher inflation rate because they tend to spend a larger share of their household budget on goods and services whose prices have been rising faster than average. More to the point, it has been argued that increases in Social Security benefits have not kept pace with increases in the prices of those goods and services purchased by the elderly, and that some index other than the CPI-W might be more appropriate, such as the index for the elderly that Congress directed BLS to develop in 1987. This is not the context within which reconsidering the index upon which Social Security benefits are based has most recently been raised, however.

Suggestions to change the index for inflation-adjusting Social Security among other programs and provisions in federal law most recently has arisen in connection with deficit reduction. Several plans to curb the growth in the U.S. budget deficit have recommended that inflation-indexing be based on the Chained Consumer Price Index for All Urban Consumers (C-CPI-U) rather than on the CPI-W or CPI-U.[2] Because the C-CPI-U typically has risen more slowly than the two indexes, this proposal has raised concern among those Social Security recipients who believe they already are being insufficiently compensated for increases in their cost of living.

This report opens with an explanation of whom and what the CPI-W represents before examining how the spending pattern of the average elderly household, variously defined, differs from that of all households on average. It then focuses on BLS' experimental consumer price index (CPI-E) for the elderly and analyzes rates of change over time in the CPI-E, CPI-W, and C-CPI-U. The report closes with a brief discussion of policy considerations.

## EXPENDITURE PATTERNS OF THE ELDERLY

The CPI-W is designed to measure changes in the price of a market basket of goods and services purchased by those who earn at least half of their income by having worked in clerical, blue-collar, or service occupations for at least 37 weeks in the previous year. In other words, the CPI-W only tracks the buying habits of the employed. This particular group of employed persons has accounted for a dwindling share of the U.S. population over time.[3] Today, it reflects changes in the cost of living of about 32% of the population.

Price changes may affect the average retiree's cost of living differently from that of the average CPI-W household to the extent that their purchasing patterns differ from one another. BLS collects data through the Consumer Expenditure Survey (CES) on how households spend their money in order to assign weights to each of the goods and services in the market basket. The weight reflects an item's relative importance in the market basket and determines how much a change in an item's price will affect the overall CPI.

As shown in *Table 1,* elderly households allocate their spending differently from the rest of the population across the major categories of goods and services in the CPI. The largest difference in spending patterns between the elderly and the general population is found in the shares of expenditures accounted for by health care.[4] In 2009, the latest year for which data are available, those aged 65 and older spent twice as large a share of their total outlays on health care compared with the overall population. With respect to the population aged 75 and older, the share of their spending devoted to health care was almost two-and-one-half times as large as that of the total population.

Health care costs have consistently risen more rapidly than the average price level. Between December 1982 and December 2010, the CPI-W increased at an annual rate of 2.9% compared with a 5.1% rate of increase for the medical care component of the CPI-W. Because the elderly consume a greater than average share of a good whose price has generally risen faster than overall prices, the CPI-W may understate the inflation experience of the *average* elderly household.

As noted above, the argument is often made that the CPI does not represent the average inflation experience of the elderly population. But, just as the inflation experience of the elderly population may differ from that of the population at large, so too are there differences within the elderly population itself.

**Table 1. Expenditures by Age, 2009**

| | All Consumer Units | 65 and Older | 65 to 74 | 75 and Older |
|---|---|---|---|---|
| Average annual expenditures | $49,067 | $37,562 | $42,957 | $31,676 |
| | | Percentage of Average Expenditures | | |
| Food | 13.0 | 13.0 | 12.9 | 13.2 |
| Alcoholic beverages | 0.9 | 0.8 | 0.9 | 0.6 |
| Shelter | 20.5 | 19.1 | 18.2 | 20.4 |
| Utilities | 7.4 | 8.7 | 8.3 | 9.4 |
| Household operations | 2.1 | 2.3 | 1.9 | 3.0 |
| Housekeeping supplies | 1.3 | 1.8 | 1.8 | 1.8 |
| Household furnishings | 3.1 | 3.2 | 3.5 | 2.7 |
| Apparel and services | 3.5 | 2.8 | 3.1 | 2.5 |
| Transportation | 15.6 | 14.4 | 16.4 | 11.5 |
| Health care | 6.4 | 12.9 | 11.4 | 15.1 |
| Entertainment | 5.5 | 5.5 | 5.8 | 5.0 |
| Personal care | 1.2 | 1.4 | 1.4 | 1.4 |
| Reading | 0.2 | 0.4 | 0.4 | 0.4 |
| Education | 2.2 | 0.4 | 0.4 | 0.4 |
| Tobacco | 0.8 | 0.6 | 0.6 | 0.4 |
| Miscellaneous | 1.7 | 1.8 | 1.9 | 1.6 |
| Cash contributions | 3.5 | 5.9 | 4.9 | 7.5 |
| Insurance and pensions | 11.2 | 4.9 | 6.2 | 3.0 |

Source: U.S. Bureau of Labor Statistics, Consumer Expenditures in 2009, Report 1029, May 2011.

Note: A consumer unit refers primarily to households. It may be a family, an individual, or a group that pools its income for consumption purposes.

No summary inflation measure for a large population group will exactly account for the experience of each member of that group. Differences in spending patterns, in combination with different rates of price change for all of the various goods and services included in the CPI, mean that individual inflation rate experiences may range considerably above or below the measured average. If there is a great deal of variation in both the general population and within subgroups such as the elderly, a small difference in average inflation rates between groups may not be significant.[5]

Suppose the average inflation rate of the elderly population is slightly higher than the rate for the overall population, but that the distribution of individual inflation rates among the elderly is widely dispersed. In this case all of the elderly would be better off if their benefits were indexed to an inflation measure based on the average elderly household. Within the elderly population, however, there would be several different consequences. First, there would be some elderly whose inflation rates would be understated by the overall rate, but exaggerated by the elderly inflation measure. Second, there would be those elderly whose inflation rates were higher than either the overall measure or one based on elderly consumption patterns. Finally, there would be a number of elderly whose actual inflation rates would be lower than either the overall measure or one based on the elderly.

One study of the distribution of inflation rates across the population found, with regard to inflation rates, that differences among demographic groups were small in comparison with the variation within those groups. Further, it was found that differences among groups tended not to be stable over time. This study argued that no one group suffered disproportionately from inflation.[6] If the variation in consumption patterns is great among the elderly and if the average inflation rate of the elderly is not dramatically different from the average rate of the overall population, then arguments for a separate index for the elderly population may be less compelling.

## THE EXPERIMENTAL CPI FOR THE ELDERLY

In 1987, Congress amended the Older Americans Act of 1965 to direct BLS to develop an experimental price index to track inflation in the population aged 62 and older. BLS has calculated estimates of such an index, commonly called the CPI-E, dating back to December 1982.

In all but 4 of the 28 years between December 1982 and December 2010, the experimental index rose as or more rapidly than the CPI-W and CPI-U. (See *Table 2.)* In only three years was the increase in the CPI-E closer to that of the CPI-W than the CPI-U. The increase in the CPI-E usually has been closer to that of the CPI-U partly because a larger weight is given to health care outlays in the market basket of the CPI-U than the CPI-W. (Recall that unlike the CPI-W, the CPI-U covers persons not in the labor force including retirees.)[7]

**Table 2. Percentage Change in the CPI-E, CPI-W, and CPI-U (December to December)**

| | Experimental CPI for the Elderly | CPI-W | CPI-U |
|---|---|---|---|
| 1983 | 3.7 | 3.3 | 3.8 |
| 1984 | 4.1 | 3.6 | 3.9 |
| 1985 | 4.1 | 3.6 | 3.8 |
| 1986 | 1.8 | 0.6 | 1.1 |
| 1987 | 4.5 | 4.5 | 4.4 |
| 1988 | 4.5 | 4.4 | 4.4 |
| 1989 | 5.2 | 4.5 | 4.6 |
| 1990 | 6.6 | 6.1 | 6.1 |
| 1991 | 3.4 | 2.8 | 3.1 |
| 1992 | 3.0 | 2.9 | 2.9 |
| 1993 | 3.1 | 2.5 | 2.7 |
| 1994 | 2.7 | 2.7 | 2.7 |
| 1995 | 2.8 | 2.5 | 2.5 |
| 1996 | 3.4 | 3.3 | 3.3 |
| 1997 | 1.8 | 1.5 | 1.7 |
| 1998 | 1.9 | 1.6 | 1.6 |
| 1999 | 2.8 | 2.7 | 2.7 |
| 2000 | 3.6 | 3.4 | 3.4 |
| 2001 | 1.9 | 1.3 | 1.6 |
| 2002 | 2.6 | 2.4 | 2.4 |
| 2003 | 2.1 | 1.6 | 1.9 |
| 2004 | 3.4 | 3.4 | 3.3 |
| 2005 | 3.6 | 3.5 | 3.4 |
| 2006 | 2.7 | 2.4 | 2.5 |
| 2007 | 4.0 | 4.3 | 4.1 |
| 2008 | 0.5 | -0.5 | 0.1 |
| 2009 | 2.2 | 3.4 | 2.7 |
| 2010 | 1.4 | 1.7 | 1.5 |

Source: CPI-E index only available by contacting the U.S. Bureau of Labor Statistics. CPI-W and CPI-U indexes are available on the agency's website.

The difference in the annual rates of change of the CPI-E compared with both the CPI-W and CPI-U has decreased since 1993, largely because the gap between health care inflation and overall inflation has narrowed as has the gap between shelter inflation and overall inflation.[8] Between 1983 and 1993, the overall CPI-E rose at an annual average rate of 4.0% compared with a 3.5% rate for the CPI-W and a 3.7% rate for the CPI-U. The 0.5-0.7 percentage point gap between 1983 and 1993 shrank to 0.2 percentage points, with the CPI-E rising by 2.6% compared with 2.4% for both the CPI-W and the CPI-U.

Although the differences in the three indexes usually have been in the expected direction, the relationships between the three might not be the same if BLS developed an official rather than experimental index for the elderly.

> Optimally, when constructing a CPI for older Americans, a sample of geographic areas would be drawn for that specific population. In addition, surveys would be designed to collect expenditure weights for that specific population, a point-of-purchase survey designed for that population would be used to construct the outlet frame, and the distribution of items sampled would be representative of older Americans. Such an index would be costly to construct, however, and Congress has not appropriated the necessary funds to do so.[9]

For example, the number of households in the CES on which market baskets are based is much smaller for the CPI-E than for the CPI-W and CPI-U. The CPI-E therefore is subject to greater sampling error than the official indexes because of BLS' limited resources. The CPI-E also uses the CPI-U's sample of retail outlets to gather prices, but the outlets may not accurately reflect those at which the elderly shop and the prices may not be representative of those paid by the elderly. These methodological limitations may have contributed to the differences in the experimental compared with official measures of inflation and are the reasons for it being "classified as an *experimental* index."[10]

## Policy Considerations

If the primary purpose of developing a separate index for the elderly is to inflation-adjust Social Security benefits, it should be kept in mind that not all Social Security recipients are elderly. Some receive benefits under the program because they have disabilities; others, because they are the spouse or young child of a deceased worker covered by the program. Thus, some would argue that the market basket of the elderly population not the most appropriate one on which to base adjustments to Social Security benefits.

Having a separate price index for the elderly may introduce complications in other areas. For example, the income thresholds that define tax brackets currently are adjusted annually by the CPI-U. If it is appropriate to base Social Security benefit adjustments on a price index for the elderly, should it also be used to adjust income tax brackets of elderly taxpayers?

Finally, as stated at the outset, recent interest in the indexes used to inflation-adjust federal programs and individual income tax provisions has been prompted by the desire among policymakers to curb the growth rate of the budget deficit. Switching from the CPI-W or CPI-U to the Chained CPI-U may reduce government outlays and raise revenue in future years because the Chained CPI-U has risen more slowly than the two official indexes—and therefore, more slowly than the CPI-E.[11] Leaving aside whether the Chained CPI-U is a more accurate measure of inflation than the CPI-W and CPI-U,[12] it would not appear to achieve the purpose of those who have proposed changing to the Chained CPI-U to instead switch to the CPI-E for calculation of Social Security benefits as some have suggested.[13] Were BLS to replace the experimental index with a newly developed index more representative of the elderly population, there also is no guarantee it would bear the same relationship to the CPI-W and Chained CPI-U as that of the CPI-E.

## End Notes

1 For the specific index used to automatically adjust federal entitlement programs for inflation, see CRS Report R42000, *Inflation-Indexing Elements in Federal Entitlement Programs*, coordinated by Dawn Nuschler. In addition, the CPI-U is used to inflation-adjust several individual income tax provisions including the income levels that define tax brackets, the standard deduction, and personal exemptions.

2 For additional information, see CRS Report RL32293, *The Chained Consumer Price Index: What Is It and Would It Be Appropriate for Cost-of-Living Adjustments?* , by Linda Levine.

3 The CPI-W population excludes the fast-growing groups of managerial and professional workers. It also excludes those employed fewer than 37 weeks in clerical, blue-collar, or service occupations. The CPI-U covers the CPI-W population plus households of salaried workers (e.g., professionals and managers), part-time workers, the selfemployed, the unemployed, and households with no one in the labor force (e.g., retirees). It represents about 87% of the U.S. population.

4 In the CPI, expenditure shares for health care are based on out-of-pocket outlays and health insurance premiums paid by individuals (e.g., deductions from employee paychecks for employer-provided health benefits and consumer contributions to Medicare Part B). The

CPI does not include health benefits paid by employers or federal government programs. U.S. Bureau of Labor Statistics, *How BLS Measures Price Change for Medical Care Services in the CPI*, available at http://www.bls.gov/cpi/cpifact4.htm.

[5] BLS, *The Consumer Price Index—Why the Published Averages Don't Always Match An Individual's Inflation Experience*, fact sheet, available at http://www.bls.gov/cpi/cpifact5.htm.

[6] Robert T. Michael, "Variation Across Households in the Rate of Inflation," *Journal of Money, Credit and Banking*, vol. 11, issue 1 (February 1979), pp. 32-46.

[7] The CPI-W population excludes the fast-growing groups of managerial and professional workers. It also excludes those employed fewer than 37 weeks in clerical, blue-collar, or service occupations. The CPI-U covers the CPI-W population plus households of salaried workers (e.g., professionals and managers), part-time workers, the selfemployed, the unemployed, and households with no one in the labor force (e.g., retirees).

[8] Kenneth J. Stewart, "The Experimental Consumer Price Index for Elderly Americans (CPI-E): 1982-2007," *Monthly Labor Review*, April 2008. (See also http://www.bls.gov/cpi/cpieart2009.pdf.)

[9] Ibid., p. 24.

[10] AARP Public Policy Institute, *An Update on the Experimental Consumer Price Index (CPI-E) for Older Americans*, December 2005, p. 4, available at http://assets.aarp.org/rgcenter/econ/dd132_cpie.pdf.

[11] In a technical appendix to *Using a Different Measure of Inflation for Indexing Federal Programs and the Tax Code* (available at http://www.cbo.gov/ftpdocs/112xx/doc11256/WebAppendix.pdf), the Congressional Budget Office estimated that substituting the Chained CPI-U for the CPI-W when calculating Social Security cost-of-living adjustments would result in a cumulative decline in outlays of $112.0 billion between 2012 and 2021.

[12] CRS Report RL32293, *The Chained Consumer Price Index: What Is It and Would It Be Appropriate for Cost-of-Living Adjustments?*, by Linda Levine.

[13] For estimates of the effect on the actuarial deficit of the Social Security program of substituting the CPI-E and the Chained CPI-U for the CPI-W, see Social Security Administration, Office of the Chief Actuary, letter dated June 21, 2011.

In: Inflation and the Consumer Price Index ISBN: 978-1-61942-705-1
Editors: E. L. Green, A. N. Walker 

*Chapter 7*

# THE CHAINED CONSUMER PRICE INDEX: WHAT IS IT AND WOULD IT BE APPROPRIATE FOR COST-OF-LIVING ADJUSTMENTS?*

*Linda Levine*

## SUMMARY

The U.S. Bureau of Labor Statistics (BLS) publishes two important measures of inflation: the Consumer Price Index for all Urban Consumers (CPI-U) and the Consumer Price Index for Urban Wage Earners and Clerical Workers (CPI-W). The CPI might seem like just another economic indicator, but it could be a powerful policy lever. Because the CPI-W is used to calculate annual cost-of-living adjustments (COLAs) to Social Security retirement benefits and the CPI-U is used to calculate annual inflation adjustments to personal income tax brackets, for example, changing the basis of the automatic adjustments could substantially affect outlays and revenues, and thereby, the budget deficit.

As part of its continuing effort to improve measures of change in the cost of living, BLS has since August 2002 been publishing a supplemental measure known as the Chained Consumer Price Index for

* This is an edited, reformatted and augmented version of a Congressional Research Service publication, CRS Report for Congress RL32293, from www.crs.gov, dated August 16, 2011.

all Urban Consumers (C-CPI-U). The aim of the C-CPI-U is to produce a measure of change in consumer prices that is free of substitution bias.

One of the difficulties in estimating changes in the cost of living is that consumers often change the goods and services they purchase in response to changing relative prices. In other words, consumers will tend to buy more of those goods and services whose prices are rising slower than average and fewer of those goods and services whose prices are rising faster than average. Substitution on the part of consumers is believed to insulate them from the full effect of rising prices on maintaining their standard of living. Because the CPI-W and CPI-U do not entirely account for substitution, they overstate the impact of inflation on consumer well-being.

As a result of better reflecting consumer substitution, the C-CPI-U has typically increased to a lesser extent than either the CPI-U or CPI-W. This relationship has prompted calls for switching to the C-CPI-U when calculating automatic annual adjustments to inflation-indexed federal programs and individual tax provisions to slow growth in the budget deficit. The "Simpson-Bowles" (National Commission on Fiscal Responsibility and Reform) report included government-wide replacement of the CPI-W and CPI-U with the chained CPI, for example. The committee created by the Budget Control Act of 2011 (P.L. 112-25) may consider the approach during its upcoming deliberations.

That the CPI-W and CPI-U are not revised makes them attractive for use in calculating cost-ofliving adjustments. Unlike them, the C-CPI-U is subject to two revisions after its first release. If the two indexes were replaced by the C-CPI-U, cost-of-living adjustments would either have to wait until the final number was available or rely on preliminary estimates that could change up to two years after the fact. Whether the preliminary C-CPI-U estimates might be attractive alternatives to using the final estimate depends on whether they are biased relative to the final number or if the revisions tend to be significant. If the final index tends to rise more than the preliminary estimates, it might make their use unpopular with those who would be affected. More generally, because increases in the C-CPI-U have tended to be smaller than in either the CPI-W or CPI-U, some Social Security beneficiaries, taxpayers, and individuals whose eligibility for federal programs is based on the poverty threshold (e.g., food stamps) might oppose switching to the CCPI-U.

## INTRODUCTION

The Consumer Price Index (CPI) is probably the most important measure of inflation developed by the federal government because it is used to make automatic adjustments that affect both outlays and revenues. The Consumer

Price Index for Urban Wage Earners and Clerical Workers (CPI-W) is the basis for adjusting Social Security retirement benefits[1] and the Consumer Price Index for All Urban Consumers (CPI-U) is the basis for adjusting personal income tax brackets[2] to keep up with inflation, for example. Changing the government's basis for indexing these among other federal programs and tax provisions from the CPI-W and CPI-U could have substantial effects on the budget deficit. [3] (Hereafter in this report, the CPI-W and CPI-U will be referred to collectively as the standard CPI.)

Then-chairman of the Federal Reserve Board Alan Greenspan suggested in testimony before the House Budget Committee in 2004 that Congress consider replacing the standard CPI with the Chained CPI for all Urban Consumers (C-CPI-U) to make automatic cost-of-living adjustments (COLAs) to federal programs.[4] He pointed out that, at that time, if the C-CPI-U had been used instead of the CPI-U and CPI-W over the previous 10 years, the federal debt would have been about $200 billion less. More recently, the "Simpson-Bowles" (National Commission on Fiscal Responsibility and Reform) report and the "Gang of Six" plan among others included replacing the standard CPI with the C-CPI-U for all government provisions subject to indexation.[5] This proposal may again be considered during the deliberations of the committee created by the Budget Control Act of 2011 (P.L. 112-25).

One reason besides slowing the growth in the budget deficit for changing to the C-CPI-U is that the standard CPI has not been without criticism as a measure of change in the cost of living. A true cost-of-living index would measure the change in income required for consumers to maintain a constant level of "utility" (satisfaction). But there are a number of practical complications that make constructing such an index difficult.

With a given level of income that constrains their choices, consumers decide how to spend their money based on the satisfaction the various available goods and services yield. Consumers are assumed to spend their income in such a way as to get the most satisfaction possible within the limitations of their budget. Because utility cannot be directly measured, any indicator of the cost of living must be based on what consumers actually spend. Any numerical measure that attempts to approximate changes in the cost of a given standard of living depends on a number of assumptions and has numerous practical limitations.

One of the difficulties in estimating changes in the cost of living is that consumer spending patterns change continuously. Spending patterns change because of changing tastes and preferences (e.g., for meals in restaurants rather than meals prepared at home). Spending patterns also change due to changes in relative prices. As prices change over time, consumers will tend to buy more of those goods and services whose prices are rising slower than average and fewer of those goods and services whose prices are rising faster than average. So-called substitution bias causes the standard CPI to overstate the effect of inflation on consumer well-being.[6]

The U.S. Bureau of Labor Statistics (BLS), which produces the standard CPI, has strived to construct a better measure of changes in the cost of living. Toward that end, it asked the Committee on National Statistics of the National Research Council (NRC) to convene a panel of experts to look into the conceptual, measurement, and other statistical issues that arise when constructing cost-of-living indexes.[7] In its 2002 report, the panel endorsed continuing to use the CPI for tax indexation, which began in 1985 as required by the Economic Recovery Tax Act of 1981. It suggested that poverty thresholds (which determine eligibility for government transfer programs such as Medicaid and food stamps) might be adjusted by a fixed percentage of median income or consumption of workers, and mentioned a 1995 NRC report on measuring poverty that had suggested thresholds be adjusted by a fixed ratio of the median consumption of necessities (e.g., food and shelter). The panel expressed support for BLS's then in-development Chained Consumer Price Index for all Urban Consumers as a means of more accurately adjusting Social Security retirement benefits among other federal payments (e.g., military and civil service pensions; veterans' benefits) for real changes in the cost of living.[8] But, there are difficulties with switching to the C-CPI-U despite it more fully accounting for substitution bias and thereby more accurately reflecting changes in the cost of living.

This report explains methodological and statistical differences between the standard CPI and the C-CPI-U. It then addresses a key impediment to moving to the C-CPI-U. The report closes with a discussion of the potential impact of such a switch on the federal budget deficit.

## Methodological Differences Between the Standard CPI and the C-CPI-U

Because the standard CPI is a fixed-weight index, it does not entirely reflect ongoing changes in buying habits. As the overall level of prices changes, relative prices change as well.

Consumers can to some degree change their spending patterns in response to these prices changes by buying relatively more of those goods whose prices are rising more slowly.

If these changes in consumer spending patterns have no effect on overall consumer satisfaction, then a price index based on a fixed market basket of goods and services will overstate the increase in the cost of a given standard of living. Because the standard CPI does not fully account for consumers' ability to insulate themselves from inflation by changing their spending patterns, it overestimates how much they would need to raise total spending to maintain a constant standard of living. The C-CPI-U, in contrast, is constructed in such a way as to better account for substitution bias.

## The CPI-U and CPI-W

The standard CPI is a fixed-weight (Laspeyres) price index which measures the change in retail prices of an unchanging mix of goods and services purchased by consumers. To see how a fixed-weight index is calculated, consider the simple case of two time periods and two goods. In the first period, the value of the index is one. The index value in the second period is a function of the quantities in the first period and the prices in the two periods. It is a weighted sum.

The first step is to calculate, for each good, the ratio of the price in the second period to the price in the first period. The ratios are then summed using expenditure shares in only the first period as weights. To see how a fixed-weight price index is calculated, see *Box 1*.

The standard CPI is, strictly speaking, a modified fixed-weight price index. That is, the market basket of goods and services is periodically changed to keep it up to date. Until recently, however, those updates occurred only about once every 10 years. With the release of CPI data for January 2002, the market basket was updated to reflect spending patterns reported in the Consumer Expenditure (CE) Survey for the 1999-2000 period. Since then, BLS has updated the expenditure weights every two years.[9] With the release of the January 2010 CPI, the weights were updated to reflect spending patterns in the 2007-2008 period. Despite this more frequent updating of the market basket, the standard CPI continues to be subject to the substitution bias that is inherent in a fixed-weight index.

**Box 1. Calculating a Fixed-Weight "Laspeyres" Price Index ($\text{Index}^L$)**

To illustrate, consider the formula:

$$\text{Index}^{L}_{[1;t]} = \sum_{i} s_i^0 \left( \frac{p_i^t}{p_i^1} \right)$$

where i refers to the good, t refers to the time period, p refers to the price, and $s_i$ refers to the expenditure share for each good in the first period. Consider also the following hypothetical values for prices and quantities:

| Period | Beer | | | | Wine | | |
|---|---|---|---|---|---|---|---|
| | Quantity | Price | Cost | Quantity | Price | Cost | Total Cost |
| 1 | 10 | $4 | $40 | 6 | $10 | $60 | $100 |
| 2 | 12 | $2 | $24 | 4 | $19 | $76 | $100 |

The index for period 1 is 1.000, and the index value for period 2 is:

$$\text{Index}^{L}_{2} = \left[ 0.4 \times \left( \frac{2}{4} \right) \right] + \left[ 0.6 \times \left( \frac{19}{10} \right) \right]$$

$$\text{Index}^{L}_{2} = 1.340$$

Using expenditure weights from the first period (in the case of beer, the expenditure weight is 40 ÷ 100 = 0.40, and for wine it is 60 ÷ 100 = 0.60), yields an index value in the second period of 1.340 which indicates a 34.0% increase in the price of this market basket. As the measure of price change does not take into account that the consumer bought more beer and less wine because of the change in relative prices, the index does not reflect substitution.

The standard CPI is never revised. This makes it attractive for calculating COLAs. But, even a small discrepancy between estimated and actual changes in the cost of living each year will be cumulative over time.

## The C-CPI-U

In an effort to get an estimate of the effect of consumer substitution on the standard CPI, BLS introduced a supplemental measure known as the Chained Consumer Price Index for all Urban Consumers (C-CPI-U). It does not replace either the CPI-W or CPI-U, and has not to date affected any current indexing provisions of federal programs.

The aim of the C-CPI-U is to produce a measure of change in consumer prices that is free of upper-level substitution bias. Upper-level substitution refers to consumers changing their spending between broad categories in the market basket (e.g., buying more chicken and less fish due an increase in the price of fish compared with chicken from one month to the next).[10]

The final release of the C-CPI-U is calculated using a Törnqvist index formula that relies on consumer expenditure data for the current and prior months as a means of accounting for any substitution across categories made by consumers in response to changes in relative prices. In other words, "the final version of the C-CPI-U is based on actual consumer behavior, rather than assumptions about consumer substitution."[11] BLS estimated that the decrease in cost-of-living growth due to accounting for upper-level substitution may be 0.3 percentage points. To see how a Törnqvist price index is calculated, see *Box 2*.

Because the Törnqvist index requires expenditure data that is not immediately available, it cannot be published concurrently with the standard CPI. However, BLS publishes an initial estimate of the C-CPI-U that coincides with the release of the standard CPI each month by using a geometric mean formula (discussed immediately below). Every February, the initial C-CPI-U estimates for all of the months in the previous calendar year are revised again using a geometric mean formula. The revision is referred to as the "interim" release. The following February, the final C-CPI-U estimates based on the Törnqvist formula are released for all of those same months.

The initial and interim releases of the C-CPI-U are based on the same expenditure weights used for the CPI-U but a geometric mean formula is used in aggregating the basic indexes to create the upper-level indexes in the initial and interim releases.[12] In contrast with the Laspeyres index in which the quantities are held constant in both periods, the geometric mean index formula holds expenditure shares (price times quantity) constant. It assumes a particular consumer response to the change in relative prices. That means that if the price of a good rises, the quantity consumed implicitly falls.

**Box 2. Calculating a "Törnqvist" Price Index (Index$^T$)**

The Törnqvist index formula looks like this:

$$\mathbf{Index}^{T}_{[1;t]} = \prod_i \left(\frac{p_i^t}{p_i^1}\right)^{\left(\frac{s_i^1+s_i^t}{2}\right)}$$

In this case, for each good (i), the price in the second period (in which case $p^t$ is simply $p^2$) is divided by the price in the first period ($p^1$) and the exponent applied to that ratio is the average of the expenditure weights of that good in the two periods. In this formula, the Π symbol indicates that each of the weighted price ratios for the goods in the market basket are multiplied together. Continuing with the same hypothetical numbers from the previous example and using the Törnqvist formula gives:

$$\mathbf{Index}^{T}_{2} = \left(\frac{2}{4}\right)^{\left(\frac{.40+.32}{2}\right)} \times \left(\frac{19}{10}\right)^{\left(\frac{.60+.68}{2}\right)}$$

$$\mathbf{Index}^{T}_{2} = 1.175$$

The index value for the second period of 1.175 indicates a 17.5% increase in price, which is less than the 34.0% price increase of the fixed-weight market basket.

Some research has suggested that the geometric mean based price index may have a negative substitution bias if consumers are assumed to respond to changes in relative prices more than they actually do.[13] To see how a geometric mean index is calculated, see *Box 3*.

The initial and interim releases of the C-CPI-U are further adjusted based on historical differences between geometric mean and Törnqvist indexes. This is done so that the initial and interim release are closer to the final index number. BLS is continuing to study methods to further narrow the gap between preliminary and final index numbers. [14]

Although the C-CPI-U may be superior to the standard CPI in some respects, final data are far from timely.

**Box 3. Calculating a Geometric Mean Index ($\text{Index}^G$)**

The formula for a geometric mean price index looks like this:

$$\text{Index}^G_{[1;t]} = \prod_i \left(\frac{p_i^t}{p_i^1}\right)^{s_i^1}$$

Using the same prices and quantities as in the previous example with this formula gives:

$$\text{Index}^G_2 = \left(\frac{2}{4}\right)^{.4} \times \left(\frac{19}{10}\right)^{.6}$$

$$\text{Index}^G_2 = 1.114$$

The geometric mean approach to calculating the price index for period 2 yields an increase of 11.4% between the two periods, which is less than either of the other two measures.

For example, in the case of the release of C-CPI-U data for the month of January 2009, the initial release occurred in February 2009, the interim release occurred in February 2010, and final release in February 2011.

Final data for all of the months in calendar 2009 also were not released until February 2011. Thus, the wait for the final release of any January C-CPI-U is 25 months. But, because all of the months in a given calendar year are revised at the same time, the wait for the final release of any December C-CPI-U is 14 months. (See *Table 1* for how many months after the reference month, the month for which the data are reported, the various releases are published.)

## STATISTICAL DIFFERENCES BETWEEN THE CPI AND C-CPI-U

Data for the C-CPI-U are now available beginning with December 1999. Final data are available through the end of 2009, and interim data are available through the end of 2010. As shown in Table 2, most of the time the increase in the final C-CPI-U has been smaller than for the increase in the standard CPI.

The short history of the C-CPI-U makes it difficult to say with confidence how large differences between the final and preliminary indexes are likely to be. In two years, the change between interim and final releases was 0.3 percentage point, a significant revision. The initial estimate for 2006 indicated a larger increase in the cost of living than either the CPI-U or CPI-W, but the final estimate was revised downward by 0.4 percentage point, which produced an increase in the CCPI-U that was smaller than the increase in the standard CPI. The interim release for 2009 indicated a larger increase in the cost of living than either the CPI-U or CPI-W, but the final estimate was revised downward by 1.3 percentage points, which produced an increase in the CCPI-U that was smaller than the increase in the standard CPI. As shown in *Figure 1*, most other revisions to the C-CPI-U have been small.

## POLICY CONSIDERATIONS

The CPI is important, not only as an economic indicator, but also because it has significant implications for the budget through the indexing of some tax provisions and federal programs. If the CPI overstates the effect of inflation on consumers, then Social Security benefits are rising more rapidly than necessary to preserve the living standards of beneficiaries and income tax brackets are rising more than necessary to avoid "bracket creep."[15]

**Table 1. Number of Months after Reference Month That Data Are Released**

| Reference Month | CPI-U/W | | C-CPI-U | |
|---|---|---|---|---|
| | | Initial Release | Interim Release | Final Release |
| January | 1 | 1 | 13 | 25 |
| February | 1 | 1 | 12 | 24 |
| March | 1 | 1 | 11 | 23 |
| April | 1 | 1 | 10 | 22 |
| May | 1 | 1 | 9 | 21 |
| June | 1 | 1 | 8 | 20 |
| July | 1 | 1 | 7 | 19 |
| August | 1 | 1 | 6 | 18 |
| September | 1 | 1 | 5 | 17 |
| October | 1 | 1 | 4 | 16 |
| November | 1 | 1 | 3 | 15 |
| December | 1 | 1 | 2 | 14 |

Source: U.S. Bureau of Labor Statistics, CPI news releases.

**Table 2. The C-CPI-U, the CPI-U, and the CPI-W**

| | | | Percentage Change | | |
|---|---|---|---|---|---|
| 12-Month Period Ending in | | C-CPI-U | | CPI-U | CPI-W |
| December of: | Initial | Interim | Final | | |
| 2000 | n.a. | n.a. | 2.6 | 3.4 | 3.4 |
| 2001 | n.a.. | n.a. | 1.3 | 1.6 | 1.3 |
| 2002 | n.a. | 2.3 | 2.0 | 2.4 | 2.4 |
| 2003 | 1.6 | 1.5 | 1.7 | 1.9 | 1.6 |
| 2004 | 3.0 | 3.1 | 3.2 | 3.3 | 3.4 |
| 2005 | 3.0 | 3.2 | 2.9 | 3.4 | 3.5 |
| 2006 | 2.7 | 2.4 | 2.3 | 2.5 | 2.4 |
| 2007 | 3.4 | 3.6 | 3.7 | 4.1 | 4.3 |
| 2008 | -0.4 | -0.6 | 0.2 | 0.1 | -0.5 |
| 2009 | 2.7 | 3.8 | 2.5 | 2.7 | 3.4 |
| 2010 | 1.4 | 1.4 | n.a. | 1.5 | 1.7 |

Source: U.S. Bureau of Labor Statistics, not seasonally adjusted CPI data.
Note: n.a.=not available.

If the C-CPI-U is a better measure of changes in the true cost of living, and the goal of indexing is strictly to reflect changes in the cost of living, then the C-CPI-U might be considered as a measure on which to base those adjustments.

As previously discussed, however, a major complication of switching to the C-CPI-U is that final data are not available for up to two years after the reference period. The Social Security cost-of-living adjustment (COLA) payable in January 2011 was based on the average percentage increase between third quarter 2010 and 2008 CPI data (because 2008 was the last year in which a COLA was effective).16 Final C-CPI-U data for the third quarter of 2010 will not become available until February 2012, however. Such a long time lag might make the final C-CPI-U number a poor candidate as an index for automatic adjustments.

Preliminary C-CPI-U estimates might be an attractive alternative to using the final C-CPI-U. If there is a tendency for the final index to rise more than the initial or interim indexes, it might make the preliminary indexes unpopular with those who would be affected. Speaking more generally, basing future COLAs on any version of the C-CPI-U could generate opposition from some

Social Security beneficiaries, taxpayers, and those whose eligibility for federal programs is based on poverty thresholds because the index has tended to rise less than either the CPI-U or the CPI-W as they are now calculated.

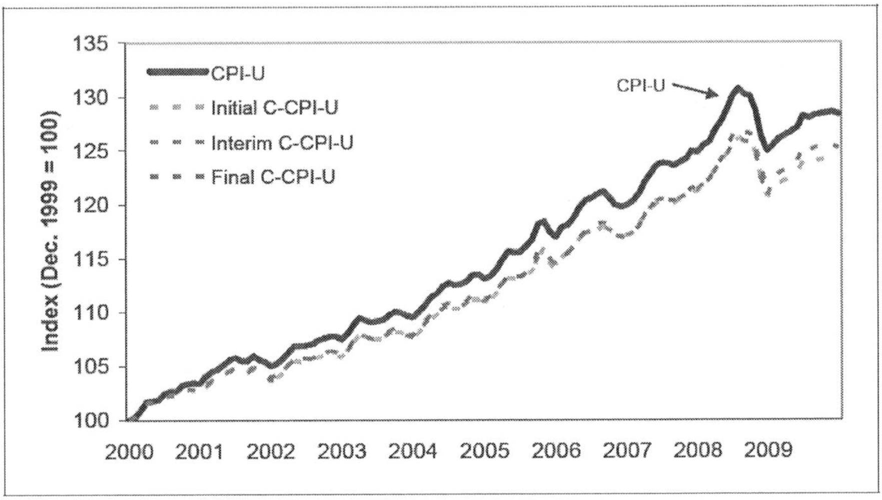


Source: Created by CRS from U.S. Bureau of Labor Statistics' CPI data.

Figure 1. The CPI-U and the C-CPI-U.

The elderly and their advocates are likely to be among those who oppose to changing the current basis for indexation. If the prices Social Security beneficiaries and federal and military pensioners face increase at an above-average rate, switching to the C-CPI-U might not enable this population to maintain its standard of living. The elderly spend more than the population at large on health care, and prices for these services generally have increased at an above-average rate.[17] An experimental fixed-weight index for those aged 62 and older (CPI-E) computed by BLS has increased 0.27 percentage points faster than the CPI-W from the CPI-E's inception in December 1982 to December 2010. However, it is difficult to gauge whether the cost of living among the elderly actually increases more quickly than among younger persons due to rising health care prices because BLS may underestimate the rate of improvement in the quality of these services. If this is the case then all versions of the CPI—but especially the CPI-E—overstate increases in the cost of living.[18]

In its regularly issued report on spending and revenue options to reduce the deficit, the U.S. Congressional Budget Office (CBO) includes estimates of the effects on the budget if policymakers substitute the C-CPI-U for the standard CPI.[19] The estimates assume that, in the future, the C-CPI-U will increase 0.25% more slowly each year between 2012 and 2021 than the CPI that is now used for indexation. Using preliminary estimates of the C-CPI-U as described in a technical appendix to *Using a Different Measure of Inflation for Indexing Federal Programs and the Tax Code*,[20] CBO projected that a switch from the CPI-U to the C-CPI-U could yield a cumulative increase in revenues between 2010 and 2021 of $71.8 billion in the case of indexation of various provisions of the tax code.[21] In the case of Social Security COLAs, CBO projected that a switch from the CPI-W to the C-CPI-U would result in a cumulative decline in outlays of $112.0 billion between 2012 and 2021. In the case of COLAs for federal and military pensions, switching the index could result in a cumulative decline in outlays of $24.0 billion between 2012 and 2021.

## End Notes

[1] The CPI-W is derived from the average spending of households on about 80,000 items in 87 urban areas for whom at least one-half of household income comes from wage earners in clerical, craft, and service among other occupations with at least one worker employed for 37 or more weeks in an eligible occupation. It covers about 32% of the U.S. population. The current CPI-W population dates to 1964, when it started including nonfamily (i.e., single-person and unrelated-individuals) households.

[2] The CPI-U is derived from the average expenditures of households beyond those in the CPI-W population. It includes salaried workers (e.g., professionals and managers), part-time and part-year workers, the self-employed, the unemployed, and households with no one in the labor force (e.g., retirees). The CPI-U covers about 87% of the U.S. population. Publication of the CPI-U began in 1978.

[3] Other than Social Security retirement benefits, federal programs adjusted by the CPI-W (U.S. city average, all items) include federal civilian, military, and railroad pensions; veterans' benefits; and Supplemental Security Income. In addition to adjusting income tax brackets, other provisions in the individual tax code that are adjusted by the CPI-U (U.S. city average, all items) include the standard deduction, personal exemption, and Earned Income Tax Credit among other credits.

[4] Testimony of Alan Greenspan before the Committee on the Budget, U.S. House of Representatives, February 25, 2004. Available on the Federal Reserve Board website at http://www.federalreserve.gov/boarddocs/testimony/2004/20040225/default.htm.

[5] Adam Rosenberg and Marc Goldwein, *Measuring Up: the Case for the Chained CPI*, Moment of Truth Project, Washington, DC, May 11, 2011.

[6] See, for example, *Toward a More Accurate Measure of the Cost of Living*, Final Report to the Senate Finance Committee from the Advisory Commission to Study the Consumer Price Index, December 4, 1996. The publication is commonly known as the Boskin Report after its chairman.

[7] National Research Council, *At What Price? Conceptualizing and Measuring Cost-of-Living and Price Indexes*, ed. Charles Schultze and Christopher Mackie (Washington DC: National Academy Press, 2002).

[8] Annual cost-of-living adjustments were linked to changes in the CPI in the 1972 amendments to the Social Security Act. The only CPI available at that time was the CPI-W. The National Research Council did not recommend switching from the CPI-W to the CPI-U for indexing Social Security payments because the two indexes have changed at about the same rate over time. It also concluded that there was no rationale for switching from the CPI-W to the special experimental index for the elderly (CPI-E) that Congress requested the BLS to construct. The CPI-E is discussed in more detail at the end of this report.

[9] The U.S. Bureau of the Census conducts the CE Survey for BLS. "Collection and processing the annual data consumes the greater part of a year, meaning that expenditure data introduced into the CPI at the beginning of year *t* can pertain to year *t-2* at the latest. ...Recognized international best practice calls only for revising expenditure weights at least every five years, and more frequently if there is high inflation or evidence of rapid changes in consumption patterns." John S. Greenless and Elliot Williams, *Reconsideration of Weighting and Updating Procedures in the US CPI*, U.S. Bureau of Labor Statistics, Working Paper 431, Washington, DC, October 2009, p. 5.

[10] In 1999, BLS began applying a geometric mean formula when creating basic indexes within which goods are relatively close substitutes to account for lower-level substitution in the standard CPI. Lower-level substitution refers to consumers changing their spending within narrow categories in the market basket (e.g., buying more Muenster than Swiss cheese due to a relative increase in the price of Swiss). BLS estimated that the actual decrease in CPI growth due to use of the geometric mean to calculate most lower level indexes may be 0.28 percentage points per year. (See John S. Greenlees and Robert B. McClelland, "Addressing Misconceptions About the Consumer Price Index," *Monthly Labor Review*, August 2008.) BLS uses the geometric mean to create most basic indexes, but there are some exceptions. The lower level category of hospital services is one. BLS judged that consumers are unlikely to substitute between the services performed at hospitals in response to relative price changes.

[11] David S. Johnson, Stephen B. Reed, and Kenneth J. Stewart, "Price Measurement in the United States: A Decade After the Boskin Report," *Monthly Labor Review*, May 2006, p. 12.

[12] As previously noted, BLS has since 1999 used the geometric mean in developing the basic indexes of the standard CPI. It is not used it in their aggregation.

[13] See Matthew D. Shapiro and David W. Wilcox, "Alternative Strategies for Aggregating Prices in the CPI," Federal Reserve Bank of St. Louis *Review*, May/June 1997.

[14] For additional methodological information on the standard CPI and C-CPI-U see the chapter on the CPI in the BLS *Handbook of Methods*, updated June 2007 (http://www.bls.gov/opub/hom/pdf/homch17.pdf); and for the C-CPI-U in particular see Robert Cage, John Greenlees, and Patrick Jackman, *Introducing the Chained Consumer Price Index*, paper presented at the Seventh Meeting of the International Working Group on Price Indexes, Paris, FR, May 2003, and Frequently Asked Questions on the Chained Consumer Price Index for All Urban Consumers, http://www.bls.gov/cpi/cpisupqa.htm.

[15] With progressive tax rates, as incomes rise with inflation, more income is subject to higher tax rates. If the CPI-U overstates inflation, then the tax brackets are rising more than they need to in order to avoid increasing taxes on incomes that are simply keeping up with rising prices.

[16] Because there was no increase in the CPI-W, Social recipients did not receive a COLA in 2011.

[17] For more information see CRS Report RS20060, *A Separate Consumer Price Index for the Elderly?*.

[18] U.S. Congressional Budget Office, *Using a Different Measure of Inflation for Indexing Federal Programs and the Tax Code*, Economic and Budget Issue Brief, Washington, DC, February 24, 2010.

[19] U.S. Congressional Budget Office, *Reducing the Deficit: Spending and Revenue Options*, Washington, DC, March 2011.

[20] http://www.cbo.gov/ftpdocs/112xx/doc11256/WebAppendix.pdf

[21] They include the amounts of the personal and dependent exemptions as well as the standard deductions; the levels of incomes that separate individual income tax brackets from one another; the amount of the annual gift tax exemption; and the income thresholds and phaseouts for the earned income tax credit and the child tax credit among other credits.

In: Inflation and the Consumer Price Index ISBN: 978-1-61942-705-1
Editors: E. L. Green, A. N. Walker 

*Chapter 8*

# USING A DIFFERENT MEASURE OF INFLATION FOR INDEXING FEDERAL PROGRAMS AND THE TAX CODE*

***The Congressional Budget Office***

## INTRODUCTION

Federal laws try to protect taxpayers and recipients of government benefits from the effects of rising prices by specifying that dollar amounts in many parts of the tax code and in some programs be automatically adjusted— or indexed—for inflation. Without such indexing, a rise in the general level of prices would alter the effects of federal policies even in the absence of action by lawmakers. For example, if the dollar amounts that delineate the different tax brackets in the individual income tax were not indexed, inflation would push many people's income into higher brackets and boost average tax rates over time, even if income did not grow faster than prices.

Many federal programs and parts of the tax code are currently indexed to increases in the consumer price index (CPI), a measure of inflation calculated by the Bureau of Labor Statistics (BLS).[1] According to many analysts, however, the CPI overstates increases in the cost of living because it does not fully account for the fact that consumers generally adjust their spending

---

* This is an edited, reformatted and augmented version of The Congressional Budget Office publication, dated February 24, 2010.

patterns as some prices change relative to other prices. One option for lawmakers would be to link federal benefit programs and tax provisions to another measure of inflation—the chained CPI—that is designed to account fully for changes in spending patterns. The chained CPI grows more slowly than the traditional CPI does: by an average of 0.3 percentage points per year over the past decade. As a result, using that measure to index benefit programs and tax provisions would reduce federal spending (especially on Social Security and federal pensions) and increase revenues.

Although many analysts consider the chained CPI a more accurate measure of the cost of living, using it for indexing could have disadvantages. Because the values of the chained CPI are revised over a period of several years, the tax code and affected programs would have to be indexed to a preliminary estimate of the chained CPI that is subject to estimation error. Also, the chained CPI may understate growth in the cost of living for some groups, such as older people.

## Inflation and Changes in the Cost of Living

Inflation—a general increase in the prices of goods and services—can be measured in various ways. Traditionally, the rate of inflation has been computed by multiplying the percentage price change for each item that people purchase by that item's share of consumer spending in a period before the prices changed and then summing those changes for all items. In a simplified example, imagine that people bought only two things last year, cars and cauliflower, and that they divided their spending evenly between the two. If the price of cars rose by 4 percent this year and the price of cauliflower rose by 7 percent, annual inflation would be measured as (0.04 x 0.50) + (0.07 x 0.50) = 0.055, or 5.5 percent. Such increases would reduce consumers' purchasing power (unless their income and wealth rose accordingly).

In reality, however, inflation as measured that way is generally higher than the annual growth in the cost of living—that is, than the amount of additional resources someone would need to maintain the same standard of living this year as last year in the face of rising prices. The reason for the difference is that many people can soften the impact of inflation on their standard of living by shifting some of their purchases away from goods or services that have risen in price toward ones that have not risen or have risen less. Even with such economic substitution, an increase in the price of a good lowers consumers' standard of living (unless they value the old good and the new good equally). But the resulting decline in their standard of living is usually smaller than it would be if substitution were not possible. Thus, measures of inflation that do not account for such substitution overstate growth in the cost of living, a phenomenon known as substitution bias.

## THE CONSUMER PRICE INDEX AND ITS LIMITATIONS

Although the CPI is not a true cost-of-living index, BLS's goal in computing it is to estimate the growth in the cost of living by measuring the change in the cost of a "market basket" of goods and services that represents average consumer spending.[2] The market basket is based on data from BLS's Consumer Expenditure Survey, in which thousands of families report what they actually bought. BLS divides those purchases into 211 categories—such as breakfast cereal, rent on a primary residence, women's dresses, and wireless telephone services—and assigns a percentage weight to each category based on its share of consumer spending in a base period. To measure price changes, BLS chooses about 80,000 specific items (several hundred for each category) and checks their prices every month at selected stores and other establishments in 87 urban areas.

BLS uses those price data to compute various versions of the CPI, two of which are currently used to index federal programs. The consumer price index for all urban consumers (CPI-U) is based on the average spending of almost all residents of urban or metropolitan areas— about 87 percent of U.S. residents. The consumer price index for urban wage earners and clerical workers (CPI-W) focuses on a subset of the CPI-U population: households that include clerical workers, sales workers, laborers, or certain other types of nonprofessional employees. The CPI-W population represents about 32 percent of U.S. residents.

The two versions of the CPI produce similar estimates of inflation. Over the past 20 years, CPI-W inflation has averaged 2.65 percent a year, and CPI-U inflation has averaged 2.69 percent. The Congressional Budget Office (CBO) expects that the two measures will grow at about the same rate in the future.

Every two years, BLS uses new survey data to update the share of consumer spending devoted to each of the 211 categories in the market basket. As a result, at any given time, the CPI is based on spending patterns from two to four years earlier. For example, the monthly values of the CPI computed in 2008 and 2009 were based on spending data reported in the Consumer

Expenditure Survey in 2005 and 2006. For the monthly values beginning in January 2010, BLS used new data to update the market basket to reflect purchases made in 2007 and 2008.

Because the CPI is based on spending patterns from a point in the past, it does not fully incorporate the effects of economic substitution. Therefore, the CPI grows faster than the cost of living does. That substitution bias would exist whether the market basket was from one month ago or five years ago. However, greater periods of time between updates to the basket tend to magnify substitution bias and to cause an even larger gap between the increase in the CPI and growth in the cost of living.

BLS's procedures account for the effects of substitution *within* most basic categories of goods and services in the market basket—such as when some consumers who previously bought large grade-A eggs switch to medium-sized eggs when the latter go on sale.[3] However, the index does not take into account shifts that occur *between* one category and another. For instance, if the price of apples rises by 50 percent and the price of bananas goes up by only 10 percent, consumers will tend to buy fewer apples and more bananas. Because apples and bananas are separate categories in the CPI market basket, the index does not account for the effects of such substitution.

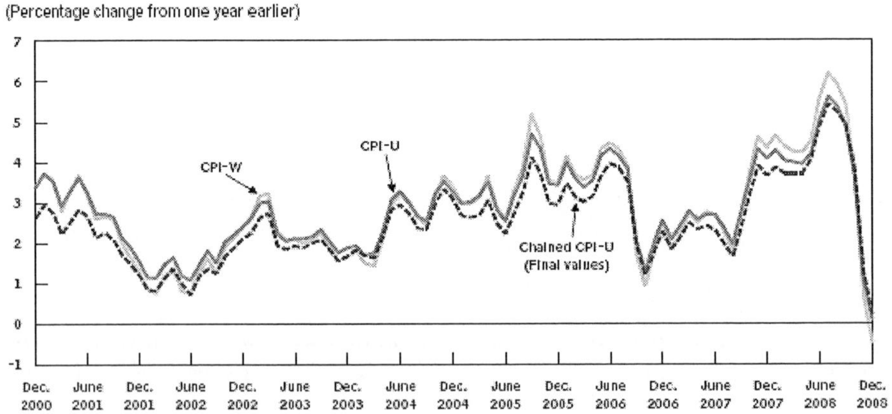


Source: Congressional Budget Office based on data from the Bureau of Labor Statistics.

Note: CPI-W = consumer price index for urban wage earners and clerical workers; CPI-U = consumer price index for all urban consumers.

Figure 1. Inflation as Measured by the CPI-W, CPI-U, and Chained CPI-U.

As a result, it overstates the amount by which consumers' well-being declines when prices rise and understates the benefit of price reductions.

## AN ALTERNATIVE MEASURE: THE CHAINED CPI-U

One way to account for the effects of economic substitution would be to use a market basket of purchases from a period after the price changes being measured. However, the resulting measure of inflation would be biased downward, just as the current CPI is biased upward. Another approach would avoid both types of bias. Since August 2002, BLS has published an alternative index, the chained CPI-U, that attempts to fully account for the effects of economic substitution on changes in the cost of living.[4] The chained CPI-U provides an unbiased estimate of changes in the cost of living from one month to the next by using market baskets from both months, thus "chaining" the two months together.[5]

The chained CPI-U produces lower estimates of inflation than the traditional CPI does. Since December 2000, when such comparisons became possible, the annual increase in the chained CPI-U has been 0.3 percentage points lower, on average, than the increases in the traditional CPI-U and CPI-W (see Figure 1).

A drawback of the chained CPI-U is that it requires data on changes in consumers' spending patterns. Those data do not become available for several years, so BLS releases preliminary estimates of the chained CPI-U and revises them over the following two years. The preliminary values are based on estimates of monthly changes in the percentage weights of different categories of goods in the market basket (rather than on a biennially updated basket, as is the case with the traditional CPI). BLS bases those estimated changes in spending patterns on measured price changes and any available updated data on consumers' expenditures.

For each month, BLS releases estimates of the chained CPI-U at three points in time. The *initial* estimate is published a few weeks after the end of the month for which price changes are being measured, at the same time as the traditional CPI. *Interim* estimates are published each February for all months in the previous year, and *final* values for that year are released the following February. For example, an initial estimate of the chained CPI-U for January 2008 was released in February 2008. Interim estimates for January 2008 through December 2008 were released in February 2009, and final values for 2008 were published in February 2010. By contrast, the values of the traditional CPI that are currently used to index federal programs are not revised.[6]

## USING THE CHAINED CPI-U TO INDEX FEDERAL PROGRAMS AND THE TAX CODE

Indexing federal programs and tax provisions for inflation is designed to maintain purchasing power for recipients of federal benefits over time and to tax similar amounts of real (inflation-adjusted) income at roughly the same rates over time.[7] The parameters of various federal programs are indexed to changes in the traditional CPI. For instance, the annual cost-of-living adjustments (COLAs) made to Social Security benefits and federal pension benefits are based on the CPI-W. The federal poverty guidelines—income thresholds that are used to determine eligibility for many support programs aimed at lower-income people—are indexed to the CPI-U. Programs that use the poverty guidelines include Head Start, the Supplemental Nutrition Assistance Program, the National School Lunch Program, the Low-Income Home Energy Assistance Program, the Children's Health Insurance Program, and parts of Medicaid.[8]

Parameters of the tax code that are indexed for inflation include the amounts of the personal and dependent exemptions; the size of the standard deductions; the income thresholds that divide the rate brackets for the individual income tax; the size of tax-deductible contributions to retirement accounts, such as 401(k) plans; the amount of annual gifts exempt from the gift tax; and the thresholds and phaseout boundaries for the earned income tax credit and several other credits. If those values were not indexed, average tax rates would gradually rise because of inflation.[9] All of those parameters are indexed by adjusting them for the growth in the average monthly CPI-U between a base year (which runs from September through August) and the most recent September-toAugust period.[10]

An alternative to current law would be to index federal programs and the tax system to the chained CPI-U rather than the traditional CPI-U or the CPI-W. Because the chained CPI-U generally grows more slowly than the traditional CPI does, such a change would reduce federal outlays and increase revenues. For example, in its most recent *Budget Options* volume, CBO estimated the budgetary effects of using the chained CPI-U for indexing in three instances.[11] Switching from the traditional CPI-U to the chained CPI-U to index parts of the tax code would reduce budget deficits by a total of about $90 billion over 10 years.[12] Using the chained CPI-U to set COLAs for Social Security would lower outlays by $108 billion over a decade, and using that index to set COLAs for federal civilian and military pensions and veterans' benefits would reduce outlays by $23 billion over 10 years.

Switching to the chained CPI-U would be complicated, however, by the delay in releasing the final value of the index. One way around that problem would be to base adjustments on the initial release of the chained CPI-U, which generally differs only slightly from the final value. That approach would be equivalent to applying the initial estimate of inflation in the past year, adjusted for revisions to previous estimates. (Details of those calculations for tax provisions, Social Security, and pensions are presented in a technical appendix available on CBO's Web site.)

As an illustration of the issues involved, consider the tax code. In the base year of 1987, the standard deduction for a single tax filer was $3,000. Between that time and the year ending in August 2009, the CPI-U rose by 91.1 percent. Correspondingly, the standard deduction (rounded down to the nearest $50 increment) increased to $5,700 in 2010.

To switch from the traditional CPI-U to the chained CPI-U, tax law could be amended to use a new base year for which the final value of the chained CPI-U was known. The amount of the deduction (or other relevant tax parameter) would then equal the amount in the base year adjusted for the initially estimated growth in the chained CPI-U since then. In subsequent years, the amount of the deduction would change not only to reflect estimates of inflation for the most recent year but also to reflect updates in the estimates of the chained CPI-U for previous years. For instance, the base year for the standard deduction could be moved from 1987 to 2005, with a base value for the deduction of $5,000 in 2005 and a base value for the chained CPI-U of 100 in the year ending in August 2005.[13] If the initial chained CPI-U for, say, the year ending in August 2014 was 120, then the standard deduction in 2015 would be $6,000 [(120/100) x $5,000].

Suppose that the following year, the initial release of the chained CPI-U for the year ending in August 2015 was 125, and the value for 2014 was revised from an initial estimate of 120 to an interim estimate of 121. (In reality, the revisions between initial and interim estimates tend to be much smaller than the 0.8 percent used in this simplified example.) That revision indicates that the $6,000 standard deduction used in 2015 should have been $6,050 [(121/100) x $5,000].

In 2016, the standard deduction would be $6,250 [(125/100) x $5,000]. That would represent a 4.2 percent increase from the previous year's deduction of $6,000, even though the estimate of inflation would be 3.3 percent (the growth from 121 to 125). Effectively, the revision of the chained CPI-U for 2014 indicated that the initial estimate used to set the 2015 value of the standard deduction was too low. Therefore, the growth in the deduction the following year (from $6,000 to $6,250) would be higher than the new estimate of the most recent year's inflation in order to make up for the understatement in the previous year. In that way, that error would affect only the value of the 2015 deduction and would not persist in 2016 or later years.[14] Errors in initial and interim estimates of the chained CPI-U for later years would affect the value of the standard deduction in each subsequent year but would not cumulate.

## EFFECTS OF REVISIONS TO THE CHAINED CPI-U

Because the initial release of the chained CPI-U is based on incomplete data, using it to index federal programs would introduce some errors, as described above. When the chained CPI-U was first published in 2002, BLS had little data available on which to base the methodology it used to estimate the initial and interim values, so it began with a simple model. As a result, the initial values of the index have generally been lower than the final values (see Figure 2). For example, from 2002 through 2008, the difference between the initial and final values for the third quarter of the calendar year—the quarter whose values are used to index Social Security and pension benefits— ranged from 0.18 percent to 0.62 percent. On average, the difference was 0.35 percent. As a result, had the initial estimates of the chained CPI-U been used to set Social Security COLAs during that period, benefit payments would have been 0.35 percent lower, on average, than if the final values of the chained CPI-U been used. Likewise, the initial or interim values available for tax indexing—covering the 12-month period from September to August—were 0.05 percent to 0.27 percent lower than the final values from 2002 through 2008.[15]

Now that multiple years of data are available, BLS is investigating better methods for estimating the preliminary values of the chained CPI-U. If such a method was adopted, the initial and interim values of the index would still differ from the final value, but the differences should be notably smaller than in the past.

With one of those better methods in place, the effects of revisions to the chained CPI-U would be small compared with the overall effect of switching from the traditional CPI-U to the chained CPI-U. The gap of about 0.3 percentage points between inflation as measured by the traditional and the chained indexes compounds over time, whereas the effect of any revisions between the initial and final values of the chained CPI-U would not compound.

In the case of Social Security and federal pensions, using a different index would not affect initial benefit levels, now or in the future. The effects would be felt with each COLA, when benefits would be slightly smaller than they would have been without the change in indexing. The impact would be greater the longer people received benefits (that is, the more COLAs they experienced). For example, after 10 years of COLAs, the Social Security benefits paid to a 73-year-old who had claimed initial retirement benefits at age 62 would be about 3 percent lower, on average, if the chained CPI-U was used for indexing instead of the CPI-W.

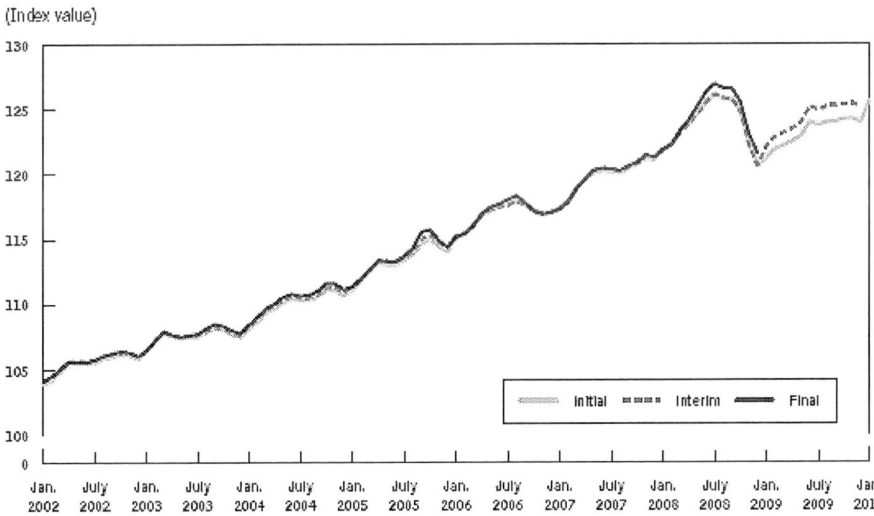


Source: Congressional Budget Office based on data from the Bureau of Labor Statistics.

Note: CPI-U = consumer price index for all urban consumers.

Figure 2. Initial, Interim, and Final Values of the Chained CPI-U.

## MEASURES OF INFLATION FOR SPECIFIC POPULATIONS

The consumer price index reflects prices paid for the goods and services purchased by an average household, not by any specific individuals or age groups. Therefore, most people experience price changes that are either higher or lower than reported in the CPI. Computing changes in the cost of living separately for each individual would not be feasible, but different indexes could be calculated for other subgroups of the population or for different policy purposes.

The possibility that the cost of living may grow at a different rate for the elderly than for the rest of the population is of particular concern because Social Security benefits are the main source of income for many older people. BLS computes an index that reflects the purchasing patterns of older people, called the experimental CPI for Americans 62 years of age and older (CPI-E). Since 1982 (the earliest date for which that index has been computed), annual inflation as measured by the CPI-E has been 0.2 percentage points higher, on average, than inflation as measured by the traditional CPI-U and 0.3 percentage points higher than inflation as measured by the CPI-W. If policymakers believed that the CPI-E was an appropriate measure of inflation for the elderly, they could use it to index programs that serve that population. A chained version of the CPI-E could also be developed to better account for economic substitution by older consumers.

It is unclear, however, whether the cost of living actually grows at a faster rate for the elderly than for younger people. The elderly tend to devote a larger-than-average portion of their out-of-pocket spending to health care, so changes in health care prices play a disproportionate role in their cost of living. But determining the impact of rising health care prices on the cost of someone's standard of living is problematic because it is difficult to accurately account for changes in the quality of health care. Both treatment costs and the value of improved treatments often increase rapidly. Thus, more uncertainty exists about measures of price growth for health care than for other goods and services. Some research suggests that BLS underestimates the rate of improvement in the quality of health care and that such improvement may be reducing the true price of health care by more than 1 percent a year.[16] If that is the case, then all versions of the CPI overstate growth in the cost of living, with the overstatement especially large for the CPI-E.

The CPI-E differs from the CPI-U only by using different percentage weights for the 211 categories of goods and services in the CPI market basket. New indexes could be constructed that would also reflect the differences in different populations' purchasing patterns *within* those categories. Such indexes could be based, for example, on information from retail stores that showed the specific items being purchased by elderly people or other segments of the population.

This issue brief was prepared by Noah Meyerson of CBO's Health and Human Resources Division.

Douglas W. Elmendorf
Director

## End Notes

[1]. For more information about the CPI, see Congressional Budget Office, *Explaining the Consumer Price Index*, Issue Brief (June 20, 2007); and Bureau of Labor Statistics, "Consumer Price Index: Frequently Asked Questions" (January 14, 2010), available at www.bls.gov/cpi/cpifaq.htm. For technical details about how the CPI is calculated, see Bureau of Labor Statistics, *BLS Handbook of Methods,* Chapter 17 (June 2007), available at www.bls.gov/opub/hom/pdf/homch17.pdf.

[2]. Bureau of Labor Statistics, *BLS Handbook of Methods,* Chapter 17, p. 2.

[3]. BLS does not use those procedures for some types of goods and services included in the CPI—such as rents, certain utilities, and medical services—because consumers cannot easily substitute one good for another within those categories.

[4]. Although BLS began publishing the chained CPI-U in 2002, it has produced monthly values for the index starting in December 1999. For more information about the chained CPI-U, see Bureau of Labor Statistics, "Frequently Asked Questions About the Chained Consumer Price Index for All Urban Consumers" (April 6, 2005), available at www.bls.gov/cpi/ cpisupqa.htm; and Brian W. Cashell, *The Chained Consumer Price Index: How Is It Different, and Would It Be Appropriate for Cost-of-Living Adjustments?* Report RL32293 (Congressional Research Service, March 23, 2009).

[5]. Another chained measure of prices is the personal consumption expenditures price index, which the Bureau of Economic Analysis constructs as part of the national income and product accounts.

[6]. BLS also releases values of the CPI that are adjusted to remove the effects of seasonal influences (such as the fact that although oranges are available year-round, they are much more expensive in the summer when they are out of season). The seasonally adjusted values of the CPI are revised, but those values are not used to index federal programs.

[7]. For more information, see Brian W. Cashell, *Automatic Cost-of-Living Adjustments: Some Economic and Practical Considerations,* Report RL34168 (Congressional Research Service, January 11, 2010).

[8]. For a more detailed list of programs, see Department of Health and Human Services, "Frequently Asked Questions Related to the Poverty Guidelines and Poverty" (January 25, 2010), available at www.aspe.hhs.gov/poverty/faq.shtml#programs.

[9]. Even with indexing, average tax rates tend to increase over time as the real growth of income (growth above and beyond the effects of inflation) pushes taxpayers into higher tax brackets.

[10]. September-to-August averages are used instead of calendar year averages because they allow enough time to incorporate the new dollar amounts for indexed parameters into tax forms for the coming year.

[11]. See Congressional Budget Office, *Budget Options, Volume 2* (August 2009), pp. 132–133, 147–148, and 186.

[12]. The $90 billion estimate, which was produced by the staff of the Joint Committee on Taxation, represents the change in the overall budget balance that would result from changes in both revenues and outlays.

[13]. For clarity, the index is rebased in this example. The current base period for the chained CPI-U, in which the index equals 100, is December 1999, and the average of the final values of the chained CPI-U for the 12 months ending in August 2005 was 112.43.

[14]. If the final value of the chained CPI-U for 2014 differed from the interim estimate of 121, the 2016 deduction would be adjusted in a similar way.

[15]. Those figures compare the final values with the average of the interim values for September through December of one calendar year and the initial values for January through August of the following calendar year.

# INDEX

## A



## B

## C



## D



## E

## F



## G

## N



## O



## P